HO Narrow Gauge Railroad You Can Build

BY MALCOLM FURLOW
PHOTOGRAPHY BY THE AUTHOR

1	Ride the San Juan Central	2
2	Benchwork for the San Juan Central	12
3	Track for the San Juan Central	18
4	Wiring the San Juan Central	24
5	Scenery for the San Juan Central	28
6	Structures for the San Juan Central	36
7	Bridges for the San Juan Central	44
8	Locomotives and cars for the San Juan Central	50
9	Operation on the San Juan Central	54
	Acknowledgments and dedication	58
	Supplier addresses	59

EDITED BY JIM KELLY

The material in this book first appeared in MODEL RAILROADER magazine.

First printing, 1984. Second printing, 1989.

© 1984 by Malcolm Furlow. All rights reserved. This book may not be reproduced in part or in whole without written permission from the publisher, except in the case of brief quotations used in reviews. Purchasers of this book may reproduce scale drawings as an aid to modelbuilding, but are prohibited from distributing copies of the drawings to others. Published by Kalmbach Publishing Co., 1027 North Seventh Street, Milwaukee, WI 53233. Printed in U. S. A. Library of Congress Catalog Card Number: 84-81743. ISBN: 0-89024-058-2.

SAN JUAN CENTRAL 1

Ride the San Juan Central

Your first look at this breathtaking narrow gauge layout

IMAGINE that we've transported ourselves back in time to the 1930s. The country is locked in the Depression, and the mines along the San Juan Central are shipping ore only once or twice a week. Adequate roads for automobiles are still scarce in this isolated part of the world, so the people here depend on the little mixed train that runs from Montrose to the mining communities hidden up in the Uncompahgre Range.

It's early and we're out at the Montrose yards to catch the little boxcab switcher making up the morning mixed. As we walk along the dew-covered ground the cinders crunch beneath our feet. Our nostrils fill with the aroma of coal dust and steam. Just ahead, the hostler is turning no. 271 on the weathered gallows turntable, and now to the rhythm of her heavy chuff she sways slowly out past the water tower.

All around us lie the remains of 40 years of mountain railroading. Once-proud steeds of iron lay in rusted mounds, stripped of all salvageable parts, their anatomy showing bare and weathered and worn. Finally they are resting after so many tortuous battles with the terrible snows of Alpine Pass.

The engineer gives us two short blasts of the whistle — have they already coupled the engine to the cars? I guess I was daydreaming. I sit next to the window and slide the shade to the top. With a quick lurch the train comes alive, then starts moving. We glide past a few buildings on the outskirts and enter the mining town of Montrose.

Looking out at the quaint false-front stores and wooden sidewalks, I half expect Butch Cassidy and the Sundance Kid to come riding alongside, guns blazing. As we clear the last switch and leave Montrose behind, the engineer lays on a number of short whistle blasts to scare a few stray cows off the track.

The sun is higher now and has knocked the chill out of the morning air. We climb steadily, crossing bridges and trestles so high we feel as if we're soaring. The country grows more rugged and beautiful with each turn.

I wonder how it was riding this train in its heyday, when elegant ladies and men in fancy Stetson hats probably looked upon the sights with the same sense of wonder I do now.

Evening approaches. I settle into my seat, comfortable and warm and glad that I decided to ride the San Juan Central.

Sharon Furlow
Malcolm Furlow and his son Shawn climbing aboard the Silverton train out of Durango, Colo.

THE HO SCALE SAN JUAN

In Colorado you can still find rails 3 feet apart and tourist lines where trips similar to our imaginary journey on the San Juan Central remain possible. The San Juan, though, exists only as an HOn3 model railroad, one I've built, and one you can build for yourself. The purpose of this book is to show you how.

I designed the San Juan Central primarily for the person who's a beginner to narrow gauge modeling, but I hope that folks who already have a pike, regardless of its scale or gauge, will find a few ideas and techniques here they haven't tried before.

The SJC is a railroad for apartment dwellers or others who don't have space for a large railroad. It'll fit snugly in a 10 x 10-foot room with plenty of space left over to let you in the room with it. As the aerial view shows, there's a generous aisle in the middle that allows you to walk about as you operate the railroad. The aisle is also handy when you're feeling less ambitious and just want to admire your creation from all sorts of angles.

I built the SJC in three sections, and it's about as portable as a layout with a walk-around design can be. The benchwork features lightweight L-girder construction and common lumber sizes that are easy to find. The scenery is all Styrofoam, even the rock castings, so the layout is light and easy to manage, a real boon for modelers who have to move from time to time. When we get to the chapter on scenery, I'll include some new twists (including twisted rock formations) on using expandable polyfoam over a sheet foam base.

I used Shinohara's prefab turnouts and flexible track. The structure kits were carefully selected to help capture the look and

As is the case with most narrow gauge railroads, the San Juan Central follows rivers wherever it can. Here we're high in the mountains, and the banks of the Rio San Juan are too steep to provide a convenient ledge for the 3-foot gauge rails.

Right. Although the vertical scenery and intensity of detail make it seem like a large layout, Furlow's San Juan Central measures only 7'-10" x 9'-11". It will fit nicely into a 10-foot-square room. Styrofoam scenery keeps it reasonably light; two men can move it.

Left. A classic Galloping Goose, borrowed from the Rio Grande Southern, picks up l.c.l. freight at the Montrose freight house. Montrose hogs are well known for going where they please and not respecting railroad property.

charm of Southwestern Colorado mining towns — and without taking too big a bite out of the ol' hobby dollar!

And, concerning structures, we'll do a little kitbashing, or rearranging of the plastic components, to achieve some buildings custom-fitted to the layout. I'll show you techniques for working character into those inexpensive kits — how to arrive at that peeled-paint look associated with unkempt western buildings, for example. It's amazing what a little paint and weathering can do to a plastic building.

Model Die Casting's narrow gauge engine kits give us the option of using plastic motive power costing considerably less than the brass imports. I will show you how to assemble, paint, and weather these plastic engines and also how to improve their performance using NorthWest Short Line's regearing kit coupled to a can motor.

We'll be controlling the trains with PSI's Dynatrol, one of the new command control systems that makes wiring simple. Using PSI's handheld controllers and throwing turnouts manually, we'll have true walk-around capabilities with no need for any kind of central control panel. I will show you how to install the PSI receivers in the locomotives and how the controls function to give you more realistic performance.

Narrow gauge railroads didn't exist in a vacuum — they connected those remote mining towns with Denver, San Francisco, New York: in short, the world. In the final installment I'll show you how to develop and use a simple card-order operating system that will keep the traffic moving between the SJC and the world beyond the basement.

So, if the idea of a weed-covered right-of-way twisting and turning through mountain and meadow draws a smile, and the thought of a small diamond-stacked Consolidation pulling its brightly colored coaches past rugged granite outcroppings sends your imagination soaring, then JUMP ABOARD! Ride along with the San Juan Central.

WHY NARROW GAUGE?

Narrow gauge need not require vast amounts of HO scale real estate for an en-

MEET MALCOLM FURLOW

IN THE short 5 years he's been in the hobby, Malcolm has become one of the best known and most popular model railroad authors in the land. He always brings a spirit of fun to his projects, and his layout photos have a breathtaking sweep that's distinctive and instantly recognizable. The dramatic lighting and rich color are reminiscent of the work of the late John Allen, and indeed, Malcolm does credit Allen's influence. John Olson has also been a strong influence — Malcolm took up model railroading after reading one of John's articles, and the two have become good friends. Another good model railroading friend was fellow Dallas resident Bill McClanahan, to whose memory the San Juan Central series is dedicated.

Malcolm lives in Dallas, Texas, and makes his living in a variety of interesting ways. He's a musician who plays the guitar and sings popular music of just about any sort — country western, rock, rhythm and blues — you name it. He's worked in Vegas and has also played scores of Texas honky-tonks. Malcolm is also a commercial photographer and is involved in several model railroad manufacturing enterprises.

Besides writing numerous model railroading articles, Malcolm has also written and starred in WEATHERING RAILROAD MODELS WITH MALCOLM FURLOW, a videotape by Kalmbach Video. The tape was made at Malcolm's home, and so naturally it features footage shot on his home layout, the Denver & Rio Chama Western, as well as on the San Juan Central.

Malcolm and his wife, Sharon, have a 17-year-old son, Shawn, who is also interested in model railroading and gave his father a hand with the San Juan Central. Malcolm built the SJC especially for this series in one year. The layout is easily transportable and Malcolm drove it from Dallas to Milwaukee so both he and the SJC could participate in our July 1983 50th anniversary conference. — *Jim Kelly*

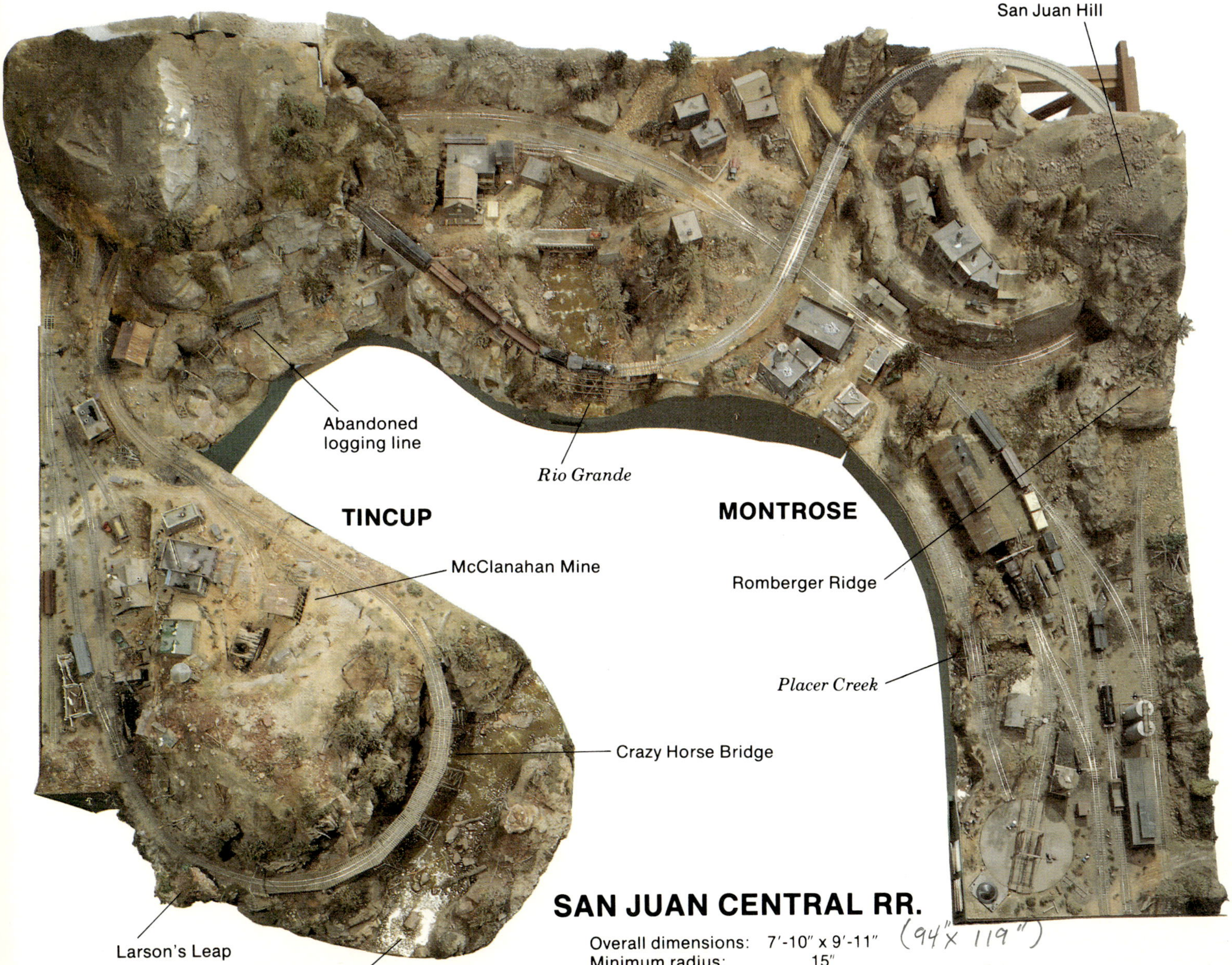

San Juan Hill

Abandoned logging line

Rio Grande

TINCUP

McClanahan Mine

MONTROSE

Romberger Ridge

Placer Creek

Crazy Horse Bridge

Larson's Leap

Rio San Juan

SAN JUAN CENTRAL RR.

Overall dimensions: 7'-10" x 9'-11" (94" x 119")
Minimum radius: 15"
Maximum grade: 3%   63 x 79

joyable layout that has a lot to offer visually as well as operationally. The whole idea behind prototype narrow gauge was that these smaller railroads would cost less to build and would be able to snake into tight places where standard gauge trains couldn't go. The roadbed is only about half as wide as for standard gauge, and the equipment is generally smaller. Steep grades, tight curves, and short trains of a half-dozen cars were the narrow gauge norm.

Colorado narrow gauge is particularly well suited to modeling because the terrain the little railroads tackled is awesome. With sheer cliffs and plunging mountain streams, it offers exciting and very dramatic modeling opportunities. No matter what type of terrain you are used to, the sight of a small narrow-gauge engine slowly making its way over a spindly trestle of questionable strength sends the pulse racing a bit faster, especially if the setting is mountainous and the bridge spanning the chasm rests on precariously located abutments.

Besides being dramatic, vertical scenery offers many layout planning advantages. Mountains can be used as view blocks to prevent us from seeing the entire layout at once. The railroad is broken into scenes that don't compete with each other for center stage. Our eyes are kept moving. Mountains and cliffs also help the pike seem larger.

INSPIRATION FOR THE SAN JUAN

The San Juan Central was inspired by the little railroads that once penetrated the canyons and high parks of Colorado. Diminutive cars and engines rode the lightweight rail of the narrow gauge into places that legends were made of — towns like Telluride, Ophir, and Silverton, and mountain passes such as Alpine and Cumbres.

In no other part of the country did so many slim gauge roads interconnect. This vast network of narrow gauge rail brought civilization to such isolated locations as Black Hawk and Como. A whole generation of westering people boarded the steam cars of the legendary South Park or Rio Grande on the road to "Bonanza or bust."

The narrow gauge lines were built to tap the enormous riches of mineral capitals like Leadville and Cripple Creek. Gold, silver, lead, zinc — all these and more were found in Colorado, and the tracks were extended from one strike to the next as quickly as possible, following river courses and canyons where they could, tunneling and running along rocky ledges where they couldn't.

But as the mines played out, the flood of goods and people into the hills flowed out again, and the little railroads fell victim to the tide. The only evidence of most of these endeavors today is an occasional stretch of weed-covered right-of-way or a small, rusty engine in a dusty roadside park.

Right. No. 360 backs into the McClanahan Mine siding in Tincup. Meanwhile the sheriff arrests a fellow for getting a little too frisky in Hayden's Hideaway.

Next two pages. A southbound freight heading for Tincup sweeps over the trestle spanning Rio Grande Gorge. Malcolm's rock pinnacles are foam castings.

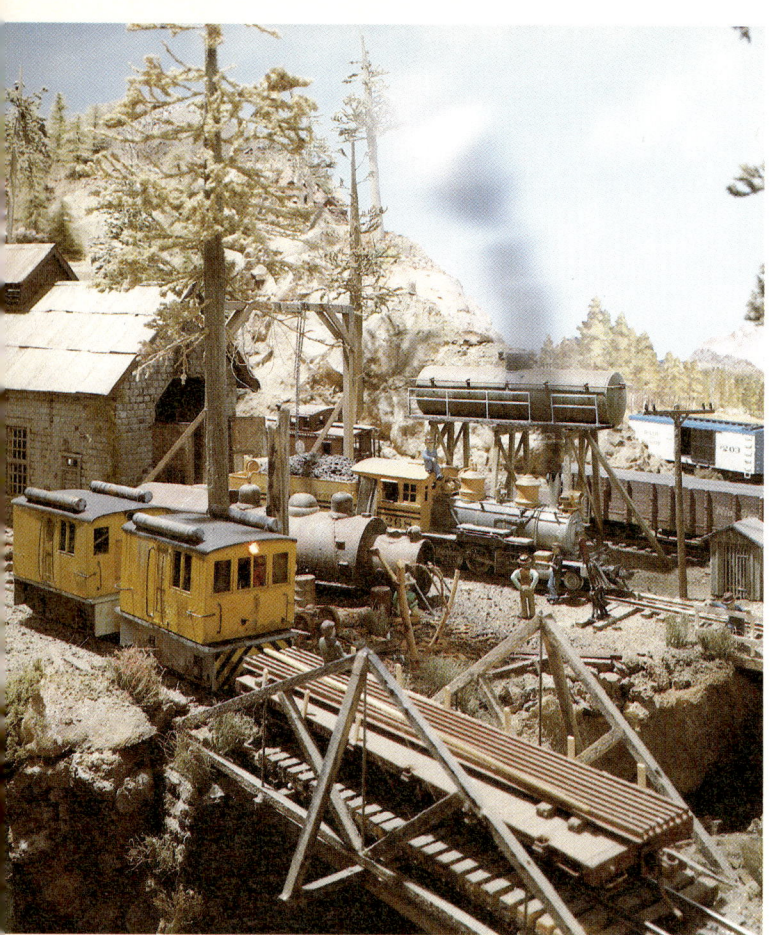

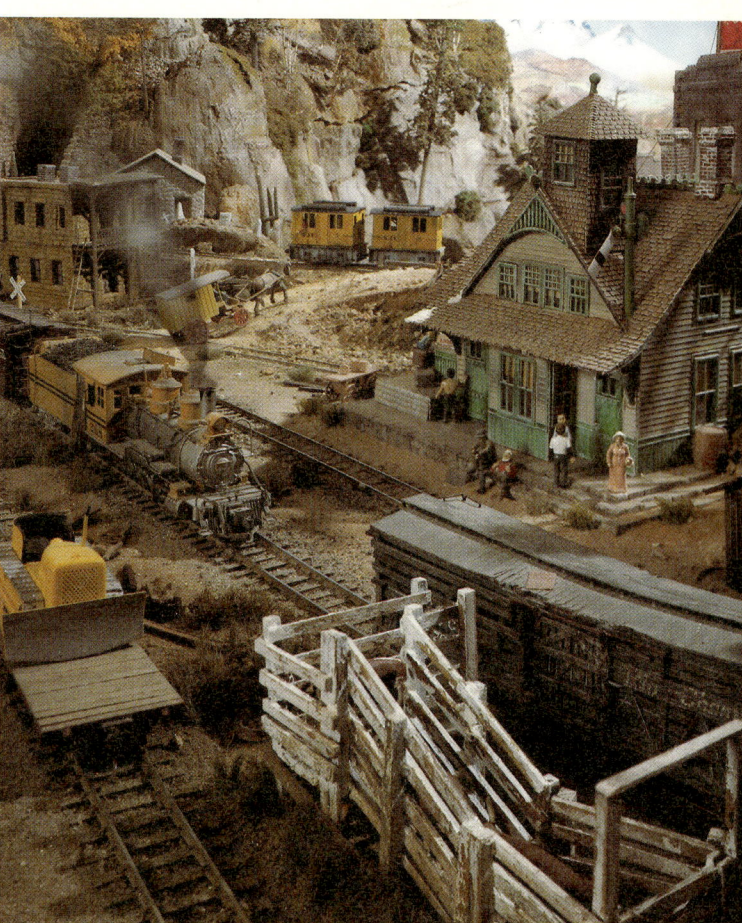

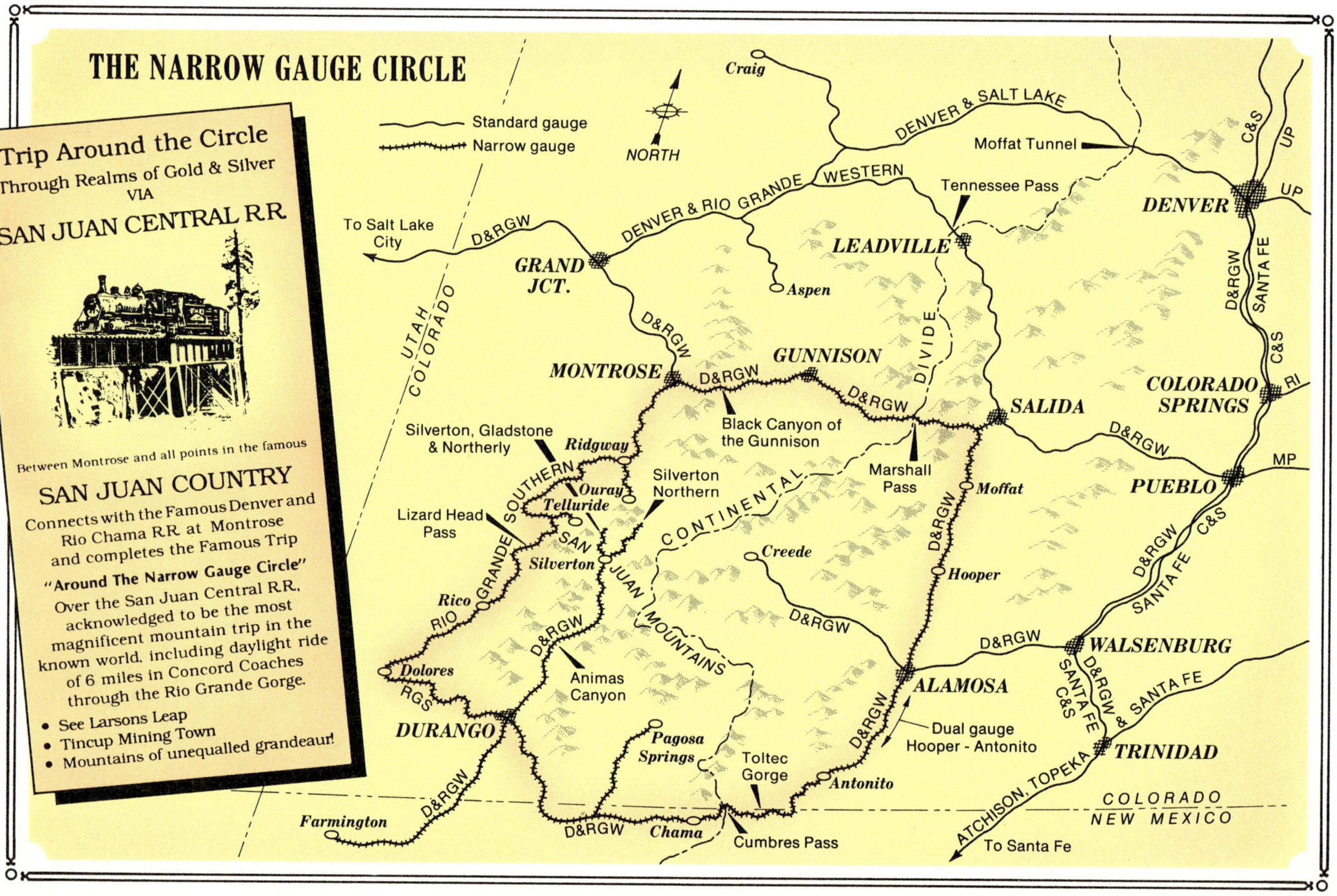

THE NARROW GAUGE CIRCLE
Trip Around the Circle
Through Realms of Gold & Silver
VIA
SAN JUAN CENTRAL R.R.
Between Montrose and all points in the famous
SAN JUAN COUNTRY
Connects with the Famous Denver and Rio Chama R.R. at Montrose and completes the Famous Trip
"Around The Narrow Gauge Circle"
Over the San Juan Central R.R. acknowledged to be the most magnificent mountain trip in the known world, including daylight ride of 6 miles in Concord Coaches through the Rio Grande Gorge.
• See Larsons Leap
• Tincup Mining Town
• Mountains of unequalled grandeaur!
Standard gauge
Narrow gauge
NORTH
Craig
DENVER & SALT LAKE
Moffat Tunnel
C&S
UP
UP
DENVER
WESTERN
DENVER & RIO GRANDE
Tennessee Pass
To Salt Lake City
D&RGW
GRAND JCT.
Aspen
LEADVILLE
D&RGW
SANTA FE
UTAH
COLORADO
D&RGW
MONTROSE
D&RGW
GUNNISON
DIVIDE
C&S
RI
D&RGW
SALIDA
COLORADO SPRINGS
Black Canyon of the Gunnison
Silverton, Gladstone & Northerly
Ridgway
Silverton Northern
Marshall Pass
D&RGW
MP
SOUTHERN
Ouray
Moffat
PUEBLO
Telluride
CONTINENTAL
D&RGW
Lizard Head Pass
SAN
Creede
D&RGW
C&S
Silverton
JUAN
Hooper
SANTA FE
GRANDE
MOUNTAINS
D&RGW
Rico
RIO
D&RGW
D&RGW
WALSENBURG
Dolores
Animas Canyon
ALAMOSA
SANTA FE
C&S
D&RGW & SANTA FE
RGS
DURANGO
Dual gauge Hooper - Antonito
Pagosa Springs
Toltec Gorge
D&RGW
TRINIDAD
D&RGW
Antonito
ATCHISON, TOPEKA
COLORADO
NEW MEXICO
Farmington
D&RGW
Chama
Cumbres Pass
To Santa Fe

Far left. Heading for a washout site, the San Juan boxcab switchers cross Placer Creek on their way out of the SJC terminal at Montrose. Steamer no. 268 has just been in for a boiler scrub and to have some flues replaced. She's ready to hit the high iron, but on the SJC it's more likely to be called the "bent" iron. Left. Colorful Rio Chama no. 268 works the stock pen at Tincup. A lot of beef is shipped out over these 3-foot rails, and the fall cattle rush brings in lots of money and plenty of action to enliven the little western mining town. Still, the townsfolk really object to the cattle pens being so close to town — especially when the wind's wrong.

Below. Brass-belted SJC steamer 361 sits on the Montrose turntable waiting to be turned. The crew got her around this far, then decided to break for lunch. Meanwhile the Rio Chama's rickety Shay needs its turn too.

NARROW GAUGE CIRCLE

In the southwestern part of Colorado is an area of rugged beauty where I have focused my modeling attention for the past few years. Look at the map and you'll see certain towns linked with a line to form a rough circle. This circle was called the Narrow Gauge Circle and was so advertised by the railroads of the period to promote the tourist trade. Member railroads of this elite circle were the lines constructed by Otto Mears — the Silverton Northern, Rio Grande Southern, and Silverton, Gladstone & Northerly — and General Palmer's Denver & Rio Grande Western.

Eventually the D&RGW took control of the famed Rio Grande Southern and ran this portion of the circle as a branch line. As the two Silverton roads fell on hard times, the "Grande," also serving the town of Silverton, became the narrow gauge giant in the west, especially in the remote reaches of southern Colorado.

After visiting this area in 1977 I decided it was perfect to model. The more I delved into historical records, tramped about old grades, and shot rolls and rolls of film, the more I acquired a special feeling about narrow gauge. Its charm swept me up and became a tangible thing I just had to incorporate into a layout.

The feel of narrow gauge is the way it looks — weed-covered rights-of-way, light rail, and lightly ballasted roadbed. It's the way the rails snake around and climb over rocky obstacles. It's the way debris is scattered around a mining camp and buildings cling to mountainsides on foundations of field stone or retaining walls made of logs. Narrow gauge is the way the whistle sounds when it reverberates off the canyon walls.

All these special qualities can be captured in modeling, and that's what I hope I'll help you accomplish throughout this book. Once again, I hope you'll climb aboard. In Chapter 2 we'll get started with the benchwork. ○

San Juan Central 2

Benchwork for the San Juan Central

L-girder construction provides perfect support for those Colorado mountains and canyons

IN Chapter 1 you got your first glimpses of the San Juan Central, the HOn3 layout I'll be showing you how to build step-by-step in the rest of this book. I hope you've decided to sign on for a stint on the SJC construction crew, because now it's time to get started building this room-size chunk of Colorado.

I wanted the San Juan Central to be portable, so I built it in three lightweight sections. I haven't actually weighed the largest section, but it must weigh well under 100 pounds — two men can carry it easily. I used two construction techniques to hold down the weight. First, I made the scenery entirely of Styrofoam, even the rockwork. We'll get to the specifics on that in the scenery chapter (Chapter 5), but you should know that it's an important part of holding down the weight of the layout.

Second, I built the benchwork using Linn Westcott's L-girder benchwork techniques, as described in his book HOW TO BUILD MODEL RAILROAD BENCHWORK, published by Kalmbach Publishing Co. L-girder has been around a long time, but it's still a fine, basic system using wood. Even though wood is basically a heavy material, this style of construction saves on weight because all the wood members used are functional — there's no extra material.

In that light, if you were to visit the San Juan Central in person and crawl under it, you would observe that the benchwork as I actually built it differs quite a bit from the way I'm going to present it here. This is one of those cases of do as I say, not as I did. I'm not one for doing a lot of advance planning, and I tend to design as I go along. Nor am I afraid to make changes. For all those reasons there are extra parts in the SJC's framework as built that you wouldn't want to include in your version.

Also, because I'm so interested in taking model railroad photographs, I like to finish off some scenes completely before even beginning work in other areas. Step-by-step makes a good way of telling others how to do something, but it isn't necessarily the way we do it. Some folks build a railroad systematically; some folks don't. The main thing is, enjoy it.

OUR UPS AND DOWNS

The San Juan Central is a medium-size railroad by most layout standards, but I made it look larger and more dramatic by using lots of vertical scenery. We end up with a surprising amount of real estate that way, it's just that most of it runs up and down. Obviously, mountains must rise high above the track to accomplish the Colorado look, but the scenery that extends below the track is sometimes overlooked and can be even more important. Not only does it add lots of drama, it helps the terrain above the track seem even higher.

With L-girder benchwork it's easy to make scenery that extends below track level because there are no structural elements to get in your way. That's provided, of course, you've thought about how deep your canyons are going to be and where you're going to put them. Unless you get into some special construction techniques, as covered in Westcott's book, the deepest canyon establishes the lowest point on the layout, and that influences how high your L-girders will be above the floor.

The lowest point on the SJC is the riverbed for the Rio San Juan. The surface of the water is 39" above the floor. The surface of the other river, the Rio Grande, is 43" above floor level. The highest point on

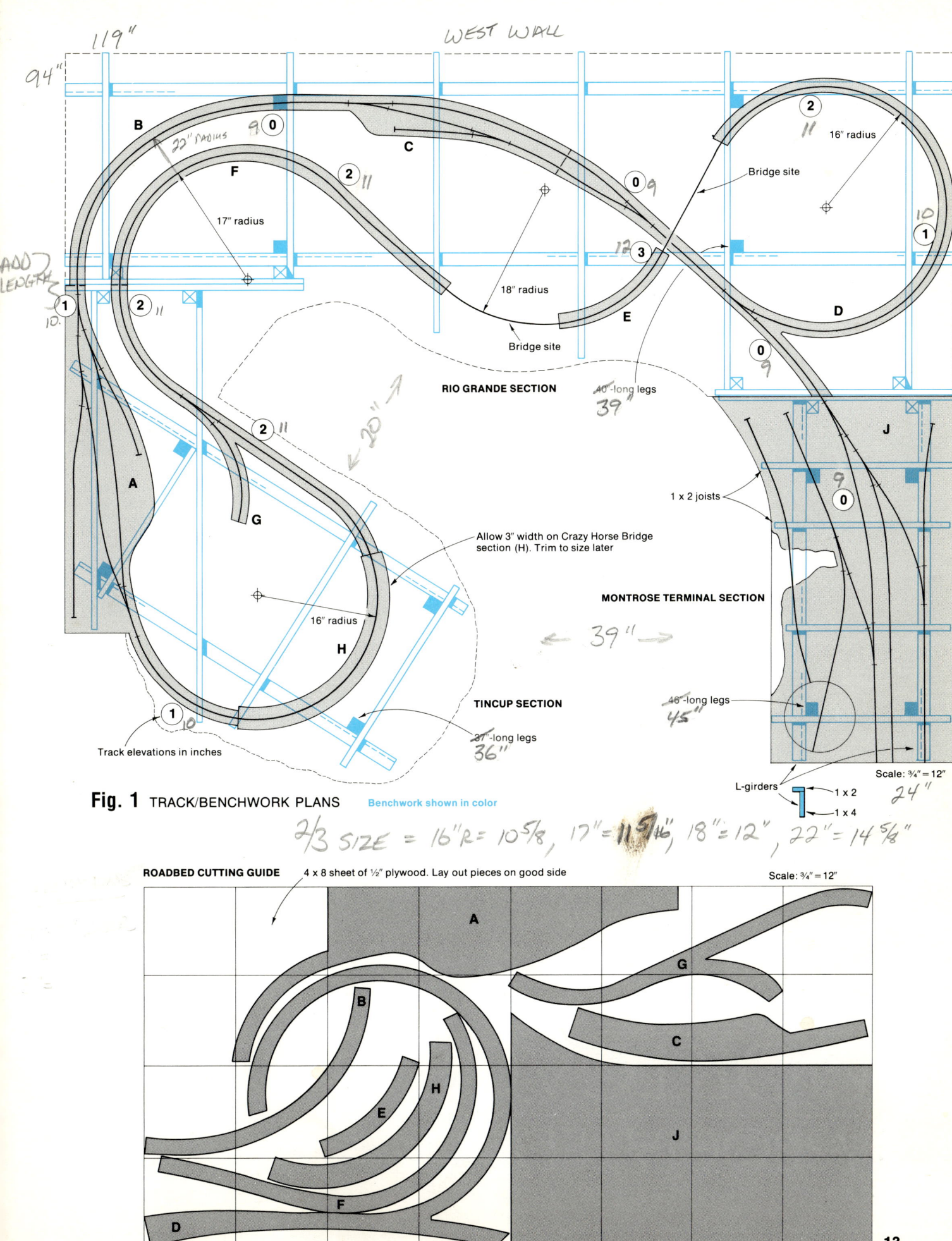

BILL OF MATERIALS		
Quantity	Material	Purpose
4	12-foot long 2 x 2s	Legs/connecting plate supports
1	8-foot long 1 x 4s	L-girders for terminal section
3	10-foot long 1 x 4s	L-girders for Rio Grande and Tincup sections
12	10-foot long 1 x 2s	L-girders, joists, risers
12	¼" x 2"-long lag bolts	Adjustable feet
2 boxes	No. 8 x 1¼" wood screws	Assembly
1 box	¾" brads	Assembly
1 pint	White glue	Assembly
1	4 x 8 sheet ½" plywood (good one side only)	Subroadbed
1	4 x 8 sheet ½" Homasote	Roadbed
1	4 x 8 sheet ⅛" Masonite	Profile boards

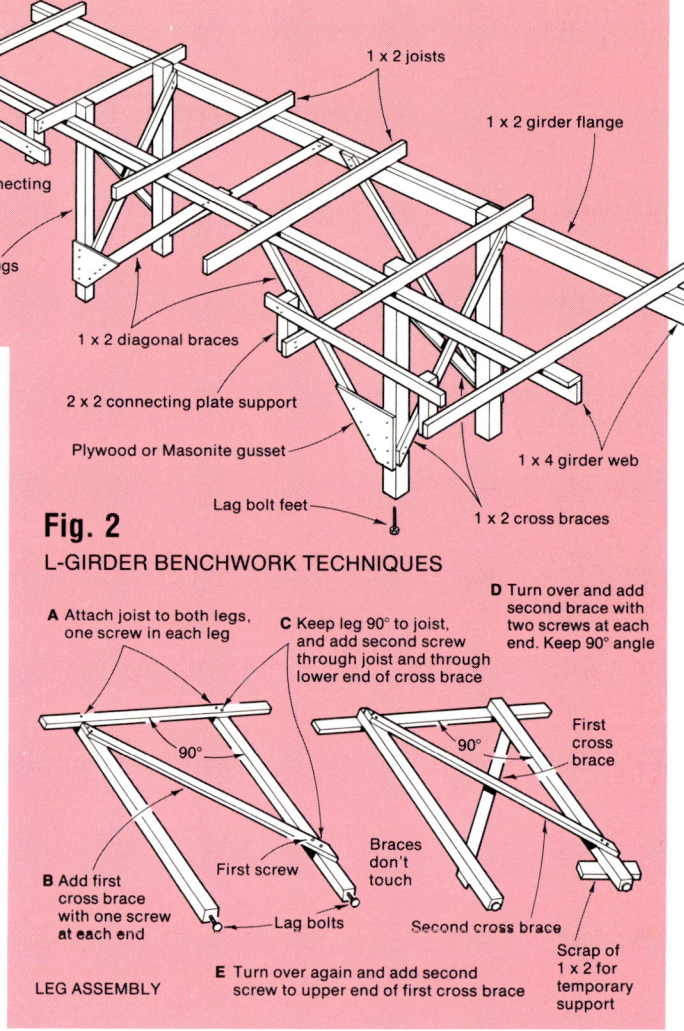

Fig. 2 L-GIRDER BENCHWORK TECHNIQUES

Colorado narrow gauge means a railroad with lots of vertical scenery. L-girder benchwork simplifies the job of making mountains and canyons.

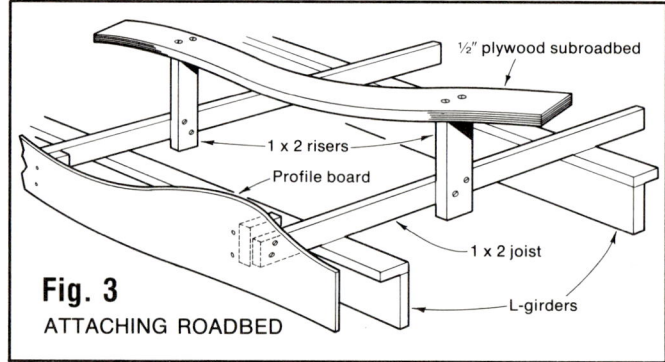

Fig. 3 ATTACHING ROADBED

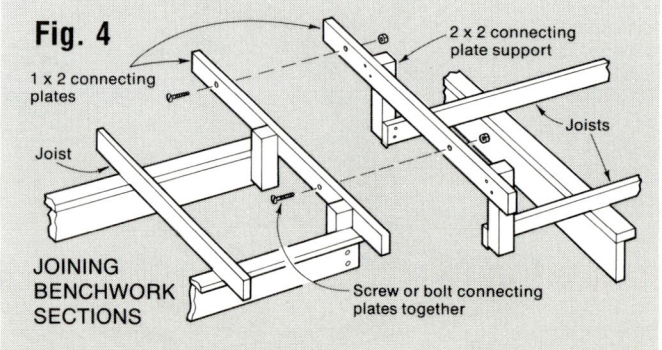

Fig. 4 JOINING BENCHWORK SECTIONS

14

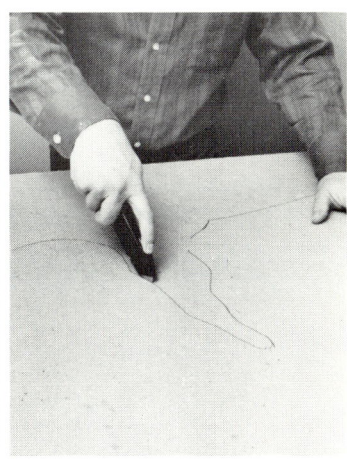
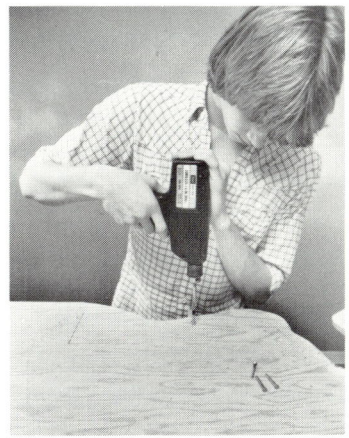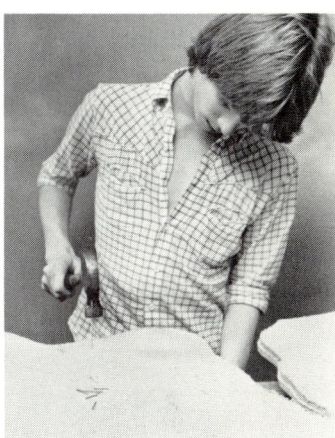

Fig. 5. Left. Malcolm used a saber saw to cut out the creek in the plywood for the Montrose terminal section. Above left. He used the plywood as a pattern for marking the Homasote. Above right. A mat knife is good for making a small cut like this in Homasote, although using it to cut out all the roadbed would be exhausting. Below left. Son Shawn screwed the plywood to the benchwork. Below right. Shawn glued and nailed on the Homasote.

the layout, the peak above the twin tunnels, is at 66", so total vertical separation is 27".

WE GET STARTED

Figure 1 includes basic plans for building the SJC's benchwork. A good place to start building the SJC is with the Montrose engine-terminal section. Certainly this is the easiest section to build because basically it's a flat table with its surface 48" above the floor. Starting here will give you a chance to become familiar with the benchwork materials and techniques before tackling the more difficult sections.

As you'll notice in the photos, I built a simple cardboard study model of the section before committing myself to lumber and Homasote. Since you'll be building to my design, you don't need to do the same, but this is a good technique to keep in mind if you want to design something of your own or want to experiment with some modifications in a plan that someone else has worked up.

The tools you'll need to build benchwork are probably already in your tool chest. You can do all of your cutting with a saber saw. An electric drill will eliminate a lot of huffing and puffing and make the task considerably easier. In fact, two variable speed electric drills, one to drill pilot holes, the other to drive screws, is really the way to go for this type of construction. I went a step further and purchased two rechargeable battery-operated drills with 3/8" chucks. With these I had no cords to trip over and no cussing trying to plug three-prong plugs into two-prong outlets.

Another great aid is C-clamps. They are the benchwork builder's best friend, so try to have a half-dozen or more on hand before starting. C-clamps allow you to fit all the pieces together and square them up before fastening them together permanently.

FIRST COME THE GIRDERS

Study the drawings and let's get started on the Montrose terminal. First, you'll make the two 4-foot-long L-girders from 1 x 2s and 1 x 4s, as shown in fig. 2. There are several schools of thought on how these should be fastened together, but as far as I can see they all work. Mine are just glued and nailed, using white glue. Some modelers prefer screws, and Linn Westcott used glue and screws, backing the screws out after the glue had dried.

Next come the two leg assemblies. Notice that the legs on our three sections are of different lengths. There are no deep canyons to allow for on the Montrose yard section so the legs for it are longer than on the other two sections.

Put lag-bolt-feet in each leg. Doing so won't take but a few minutes, and you'll really appreciate these feet if you ever do move the layout and need to get it evened up again. You can just run the bolt in or out to lengthen or shorten a particular leg.

Now we're ready to attach the L-girders to the leg assemblies, as shown in fig. 3. Use your C-clamps to hold the pieces together while you're getting them squared up. The benchwork will seem wobbly at this point, but when you add the diagonal bracing the assembly will be quite sturdy. Everything you've done to this point will be repeated in building the other two benchwork sections. Figure 4 shows a method for joining these sections built at different heights.

Fig. 6. Malcolm doesn't approach layout building systematically. He did quite a bit of finish work on the engine terminal section before even building the benchwork for the others. The inset photo shows how adding the profile board quickly gave a more finished look to the creek area.

A CREEK FOR MONTROSE

Figure 5 shows how I cut out the creek bed in the plywood top before screwing it to the top of the terminal section benchwork. Don't worry about marking and cutting your plywood the exact same way I did. No one's going to send a hit squad out after you if your creek bed doesn't look exactly like mine.

Next came the 2 x 4-foot Homasote top. Homasote is a pressed paper product I used for roadbed throughout the SJC project. It has good sound-deadening qualities and is easy to drive track-mounting spikes into. You can glue it to the plywood with a white glue (like Elmer's Glue-All), then drive in small brads (¾") to help hold it tightly against the plywood while the glue dries. Just don't drive the brads in too far or you'll create little craters that raise havoc with track laying.

As you can see in the photos, I laid the track and did some preliminary scenery and structure work on the terminal section before moving on to the rest of the project. I don't like to have to wait to see how things are going to turn out.

Figure 6 shows how I attached the Masonite profile board to the terminal section. Most modelers like tempered Masonite, but I prefer the untempered kind because I find it easier to bend.

JOISTS, RISERS, AND PLYWOOD SUBROADBED

With some basic benchwork building experience behind us, we're ready to build one of the more difficult sections. The logical choice is the long Rio Grande section, simply because it connects to the section we've already built.

It'll be easiest for you to build the Rio Grande section all at once, but as you can tell from the photos, I first built the Montrose end of my Rio Grande section, working with the benchwork supported by sawhorses. Later I added the other end and the legs. You don't need to do the same, because you have a big advantage over me — you know where you're going!

No more easy flattop tables. On the big Rio Grande section the track goes up and down and all around, and we'll support it above the benchwork with a series of joists and risers. Figure 3 shows the basic principles involved.

Our subroadbed is ½" plywood (good one side only), cut to shape, then supported on the risers. Figure 1 shows the track eleva-

Fig. 7. Above. Malcolm clamped a board to the subroadbed already in place to properly locate risers and roadbed on the other side of the gap for the bridge. Below. The bridge is fitted into position. The reader who wants to get trains running right away can lay the roadbed continuously and cut out a gap for the bridge later. Right. Malcolm used corrugated cardboard to rough in a road, and he roughed in some scenery with sheet Styrofoam.

tions. These are not absolutely critical, and all you have to do is stay in the ballpark. The one critical concern is that there be sufficient clearance where the tracks cross above and below one another.

You can make paper templates for all the subroadbed sections needed and then play with these on the plywood, making adjustments so as to minimize the amount of plywood wasted. Figure 1 includes a cutting diagram that will allow you to cut all your roadbed pieces from a single sheet of plywood, a job best done with a powered saber saw. As a general rule you'll be cutting the roadbed 2" wide where the railroad is single-tracked. You'll have enough scraps left over to make splice plates for joining sections together.

Splice plates, incidentally, should be long enough to hold the pieces of plywood firmly in the same plane — a foot long is good. Glue the splice plates in position and clamp them firmly until the glue sets. You can sand down any slight mismatch in the height of the two pieces being joined.

Here's where your C-clamps come in mighty handy again. You can get a long section of roadbed in position, then make sure everything is right before screwing the risers to the joists permanently. Keep in mind that the joists shown on the plan are just for starters. If you think other joists are needed in other places, then feel free to put them in. Keep in mind too that the joists don't have to be at right angles to the L-girders. If placing a joist on an angle will work better in a certain situation, then do it that way.

In his book on benchwork, Linn Westcott recommended mounting a 1" x 1" cleat to the top of each riser, then securing the risers to the bottom of the roadbed with screws up through the bottoms of the cleats. This is quite a bit of extra work, and I decided not to use such cleats on the SJC. They are still a good idea, though, especially if you like to make lots of changes. It's a lot easier to remove a screw from under the layout than to go rooting for one that's buried in the scenery.

A few tips. Figure 7 shows how you can clamp a piece of wood across a span that will eventually be filled by a bridge so that the transitions from roadbed to bridge deck will be nice and smooth. Also, tall, spindly Crazy Horse Bridge is easier to make than it looks. The deck is just our plywood and Homasote roadbed with plastic bridge girders glued to the sides. Make sure you make the roadbed for this bridge, labeled piece H in the drawings, nice and wide, about 3", so you'll be able to trim it in straight segments when you finish the job later.

HOMASOTE ROADBED

Once the plywood subroadbed is in place, we're ready to start with the Homasote roadbed to which the track will actually be fastened. You can use your paper patterns again or you can lay pieces of Homasote directly on the plywood and outline the shapes from below with a pencil. Be careful to stagger your joints. You don't want the joints in the Homasote coming directly over the spliced joints in the plywood.

Cut the Homasote in a well-ventilated area — like outdoors! Once you start sawing fine particles of gray dust go everywhere — up your nose, in your eyes, and worst of all, in your lungs. Wear a dust mask, available at hardware stores for only a few dollars, or a surgical mask. Inexpensive plastic goggles will keep the stuff out of your eyes.

One way to avoid the dust problem altogether is to cut the Homasote with a razor knife or a matt knife, although you'll find this takes a lot of energy. You can also mount a knife-edged blade in your saw instead of a blade with teeth. The going will be slower but cleaner.

I cemented the Homasote roadbed to the plywood subroadbed with white glue, using wood blocks and C-clamps to clamp it down until the glue sets.

That's it for benchwork. These are the basic techniques that will get you started on building a San Juan Central of your own. When your benchwork is complete (or when you're tired of building benchwork and want to do something else for a while), Chapter 3 tells how to lay track. ☼

The San Juan Central's boxcabs spot a newly acquired ex-Gorre & Daphetid observation car on the Montrose turntable. The SJC may never get around to repainting the car.

Track for the San Juan Central

With tips for making an HOn3 layout that's derailment-free

BACK a few pages I went into how to build sturdy L-girder benchwork for the San Juan Central, our Colorado 3-foot gauge railroad. Now the wood and Homasote right-of-way stands ready, and our next task is to lay the track. In a way, this is the most important aspect of building any model railroad — and that makes this the most important chapter in this book. The colorful scenery we'll build later will give the layout lots of drama, but if the trains don't run well we'll have built an attractive static display instead of an animated, operating model railroad.

If any one element of a model railroad has to be right, it's the trackwork, and that counts double when we're talking narrow gauge. Those HOn3 cars and engines are generally lighter than standard gauge, so they bounce a hair higher when they hit rough spots. Also, on a narrow gauge railroad we usually find tighter curves and steeper grades, and these tend to torment the equipment and cause derailments. If we take a little extra care, though, there's no reason why our slim gauge pike shouldn't run just as well as a good standard gauge line, which is to say just about perfect.

● Check the gauge. The first principle of trackwork is that the rails be pretty much the same distance apart all along the way, and that the wheels be spaced the right distance apart on their axles. You can't get more basic than that, but how quickly we forget!

The Shinohara track we're using is very high quality and conforms to the standards set by the National Model Railroad Association. Still, never just assume every section of track is in gauge. Check the track before you lay it, and check it again after. Be especially sure to check the curves and turnouts.

I recommend you visit your hobby shop, buy a few track gauges, and use them. Kadee's three-point gauge is one that I've used with success. These also double as heatsinks when I'm soldering rail and help keep the plastic ties from melting. Later on we'll be handlaying a little bit of track, and then these gauges will be a must.

● Keep the transitions smoooooth. Be sure all the rail ends mate well without any kinks or dips. Make sure the grades

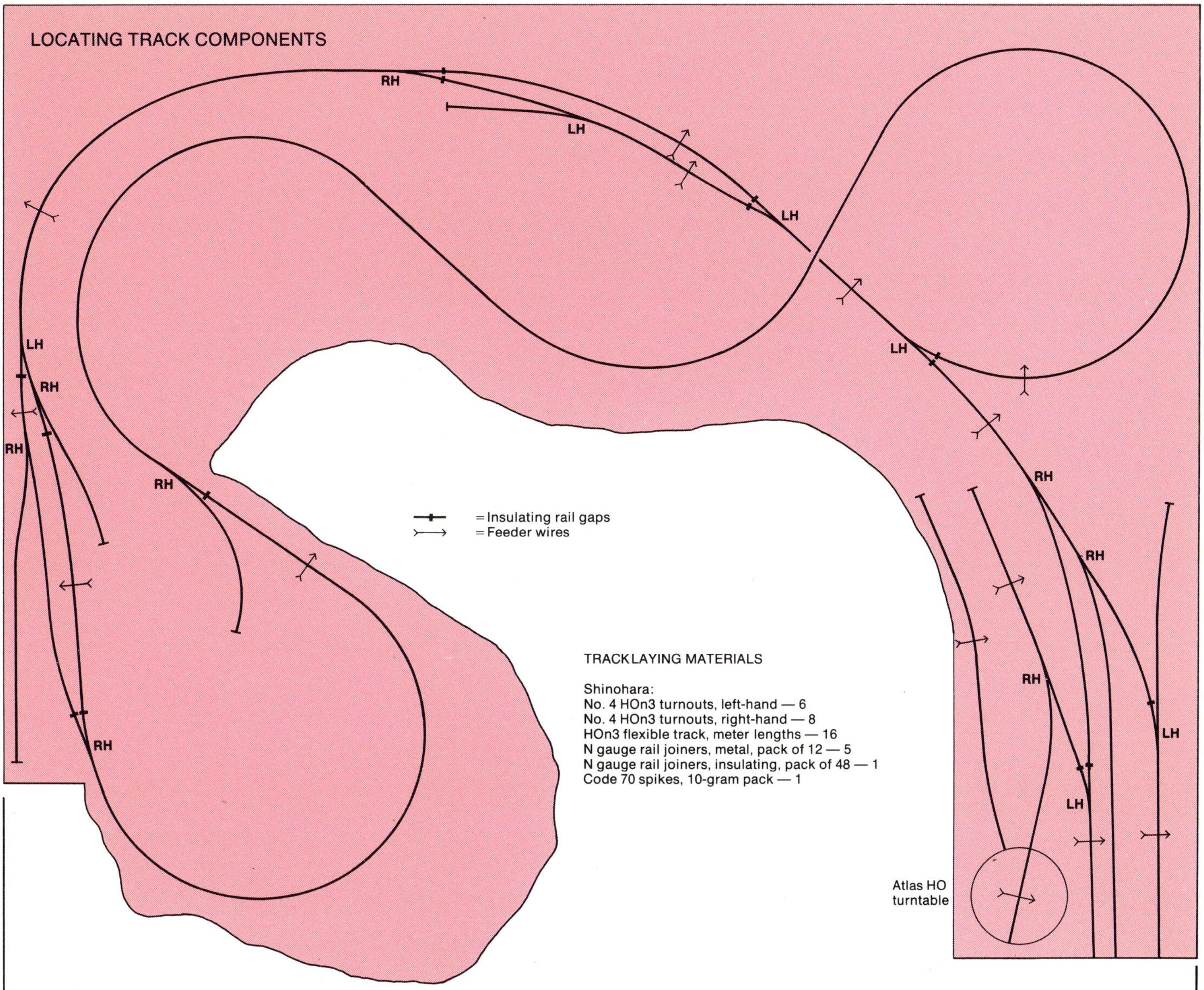

LOCATING TRACK COMPONENTS

- ■—■ = Insulating rail gaps
- ⟩——→ = Feeder wires

TRACKLAYING MATERIALS

Shinohara:
No. 4 HOn3 turnouts, left-hand — 6
No. 4 HOn3 turnouts, right-hand — 8
HOn3 flexible track, meter lengths — 16
N gauge rail joiners, metal, pack of 12 — 5
N gauge rail joiners, insulating, pack of 48 — 1
Code 70 spikes, 10-gram pack — 1

Atlas HO turntable

Fig. 1 QUICK-AND-EASY TRANSITION CURVES

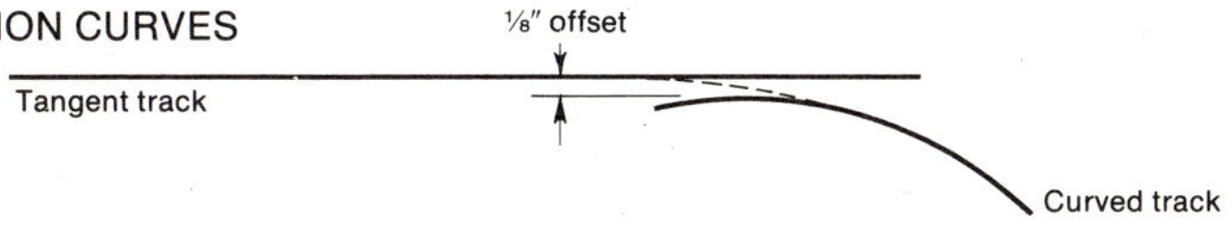

⅛" offset
Tangent track
Curved track

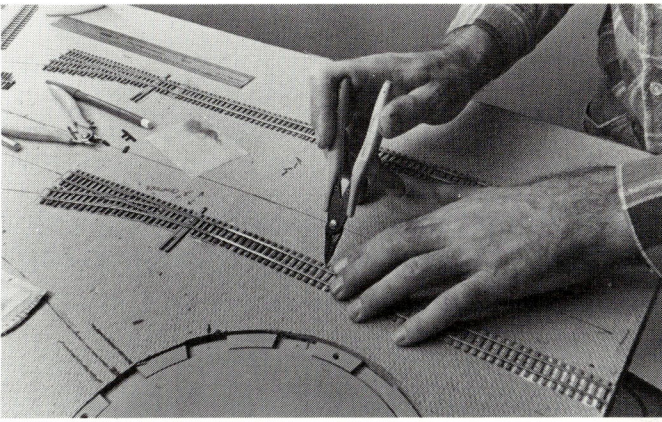

Fig. 2. Above. A little white glue, Elmer's in this case, will not only help secure the track, but will also seal the Homasote under it. **Above right.** Only a few spikes are needed to pin the track down. The matte medium used later to bond the ballast will also contribute to holding the track in place.

begin and end smoothly. Smooth vertical curves are just as important as the horizontal ones.

I like to use transition curves where straight track enters a bend. These lead an engine into the curve gently rather than forcing it to sort of jump around a corner. You can cut a template or two out of cardstock to use in laying out transition curves, but you really don't have to go to even that much work. As fig. 1 shows, allowing a 1/8" offset between the tangent lines and the curve lines will provide for a suitable free-form curve when the track is bent.

LAYING TRACK

We drew center lines for much of the track when we cut out the roadbed, but there's still the Montrose yard track to be located. Draw the track plan, full-size, on the Homasote with a felt-tipped pen. I used the turnouts themselves as templates, tracing around them, ties and all.

I used Shinohara's prefabricated track, and I heartily endorse it unless you really enjoy laying your own. Flexible track is easier to work with and can be made to look as good as handlaid. It's all in how you paint and weather it.

After drawing the track plan on the Homasote, lay out the track components and do a little preliminary cutting and fitting. There's no law against trimming back the rails in turnouts, and you may do so in a place or two to get a better fit. Once you're happy with a turnout's position, tack it down with Code 70 spikes. Next cut and fit the flexible track that goes between turnouts. As shown in fig. 2, I use Elmer's glue along with the spikes to secure the track.

You can cut rail with a razor saw, rail nippers, or do as I do and use a Dremel motor tool with a cut-off disk, as shown in fig. 3. A motor tool is definitely the quick way to cut rail, but be sure to wear goggles. This wheel throws very fine metal chips that could get in your eyes.

You will probably have to remove one or two of the plastic ties at the end of cut-off track so the rail joiners will fit properly. As shown in fig. 4, cut down through the plastic under the rail, using a sharp no. 11 blade in an X-acto knife. Save the ties. Later you can trim off the cast-on spikes and slide them under the rail joints to fill the gaps. Shinohara doesn't offer HOn3 rail joiners, but you can use N gauge ones — I did!

Most Shinohara track has little holes in the ties for spikes, but if you need a hole in a place where one isn't provided, use a no. 60 drill bit in a pin vise. You don't need an overabundance of spikes; just use enough to hold the track in good alignment. The matte medium you'll use to bond the ballast will hold the track securely, so a lot of spikes aren't needed.

Drive the spikes with a needle-nose pliers or a small wire cutter. Grasp the spike in the middle and poke it through the hole in the tie. Shift the jaws to the spike head to drive it home. Don't get macho about it — pushing the spikes in too far may bend the plastic tie strip and cause the rails to lean in toward one another, making the gauge too tight.

After you've spiked down some track,

Fig. 3. Malcolm prefers a cut-off disk in a motor tool for cutting rail. The disk is extremely efficient but throws tiny metal particles and should be used only while wearing protective eye wear.

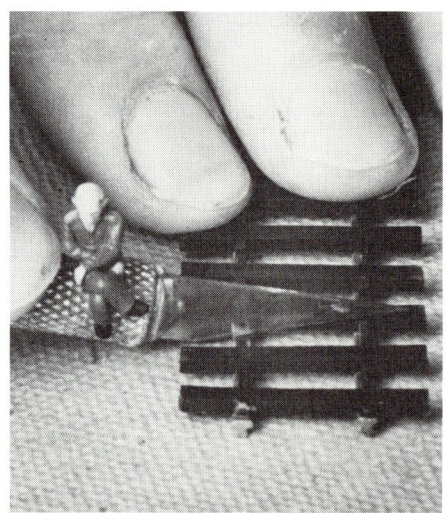

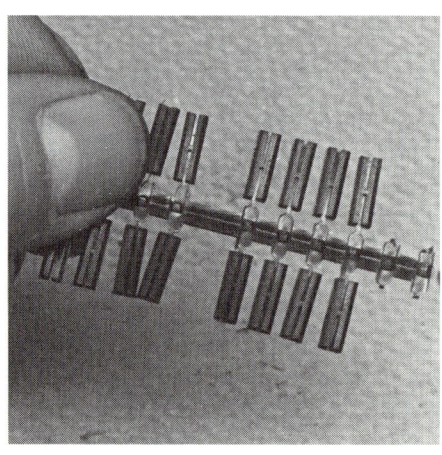

Fig. 4. Top. To make room for the rail joiners, it's usually necessary to remove a tie or two once the track has been cut. **Above.** Plastic rail joiners like these make it easy to insulate the rail.

get your head right down on it and sight along the rail tops to check alignment. Narrow gauge rail was seldom perfectly straight, so a little jog here and there adds character — just make sure your jogs aren't too severe.

Don't forget to keep checking with that gauge! On turnouts, be sure the points fit flush against the stock rails. File the point ends so they won't catch any wheel flanges, and check to see that the point heels line up smoothly with the closure rails when the points are moved from one position to another. See fig. 5.

Use an NMRA narrow gauge standards gauge to check wing rails, guard rails, and point heels. You want to make sure your flangeways are the proper width. Also, once the track has progressed this far you'll want to start checking each section by rolling a car or a set of trucks through it. Use a needle file to smooth any rough spots.

ELECTRICAL GAPS

The SJC is wired for command control, but that doesn't let me off the hook when it comes to insulated gaps in the rail. That old rule for live-frog turnouts still holds — you must insulate them at the frog end, as shown in fig. 6. The track plan shows you where the insulated gaps go. Any of you building the SJC for a conventional control system will need these same gaps.

To provide for insulated gaps you can install plastic joiners as you go along, or you can lay all the track with metal joiners and then come back and cut gaps in the rail with a cut-off disk in a motor tool. The latter method gives you more freedom in where you put a gap but has a built-in problem. The rails can expand or shift until they close the gap and short out the railroad. To prevent that, epoxy a small styrene shim between the rail ends, as shown in fig 7. Trim the shim to shape with an X-acto blade after the epoxy dries.

SOLDERING THE RAILS

I'm a firm believer in soldering the rail joints on curved sections. This ensures a smooth flow in the places where derailments are most likely to occur. I find it best to solder the sections together while they are still straight, then bend them. I start bending the track an inch or two at a time, not all at once, and I keep working the section until I have a satisfactory curve.

Where you have a section of straight track entering a curve, cut the track about 8" into the bend and solder on a new straight section. Keep laying until you're 8" from the end again and solder on another straight section.

When soldering rail, first apply a liquid or paste resin flux to the rail joint. Flux will make the solder flow much more readily, even if you're using a resin-core solder. Don't use an acid flux as it is quite likely to cause corrosion.

Let the soldering gun tip heat up good and then touch the tip to the rail joiner. At the same time touch the solder to the rail. The solder will flow very quickly and smoothly, and a good, tight bond will result.

If you live in an area of temperature extremes, or if your layout room gets very hot, then you'll need to leave some joints unsoldered to allow for expansion and contraction of the rails. This you can do on the straightaways. Leave a gap of around 1/32" at the rail joiner and add a flexible jumper wire to maintain electrical continuity.

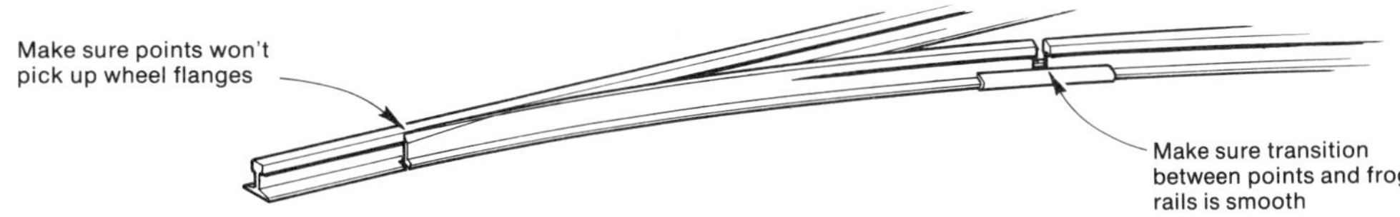

Fig. 5 TUNING TURNOUTS

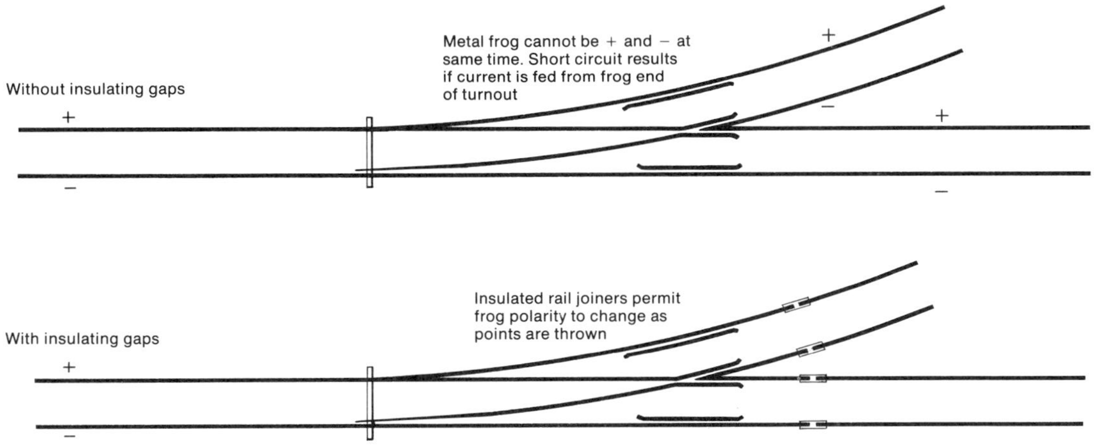

Fig. 6 INSULATING LIVE-FROG TURNOUTS

Fig. 7 INSULATING GAPS WITHOUT RAIL JOINERS

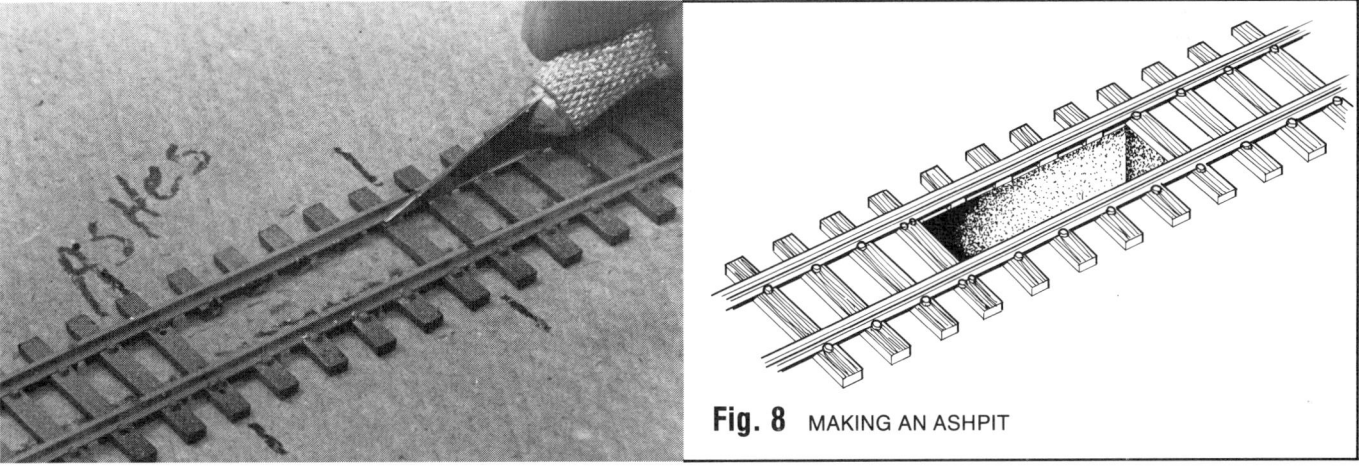

Fig. 8 MAKING AN ASHPIT

TRACK DETAILS

The turnouts on the yard and Tincup sections are thrown manually, using Caboose Industries ground throws. I used ½" brads to secure the ground throws to the Homasote. Before placing the nails, center the turnout points and position the throw's handle straight up. Drive in the nails, using a nail set, and check for equal throwbar travel in both positions. You can make fine adjustments by tapping the nail heads laterally, using the nail set. (The turnouts on the Rio Grande section are thrown with electric rotary machines, and I'll cover those in the next installment.)

The track outside the enginehouse is a good place to locate the ash pit. As shown in fig. 8, use an X-acto knife with a no. 11 blade to trim away an appropriate number of ties between the rails. Cut away enough Homasote to form the ash pit and paint it black or line it with brick paper.

Painting the rail will make it look much more realistic. As shown in fig. 9, I use Floquil's Roof Brown applied with a small brush. I also paint some of the ties so they won't all look the same. I

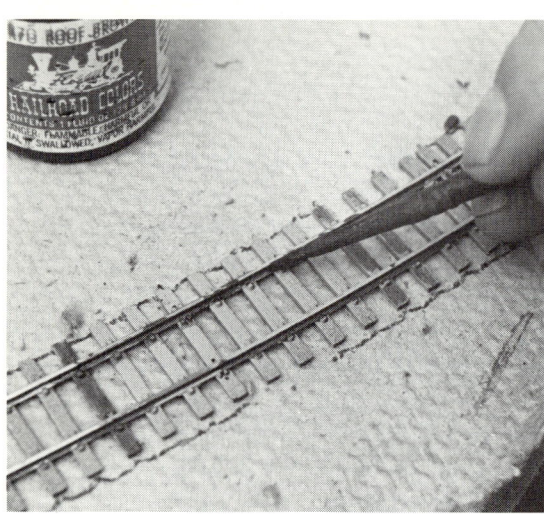
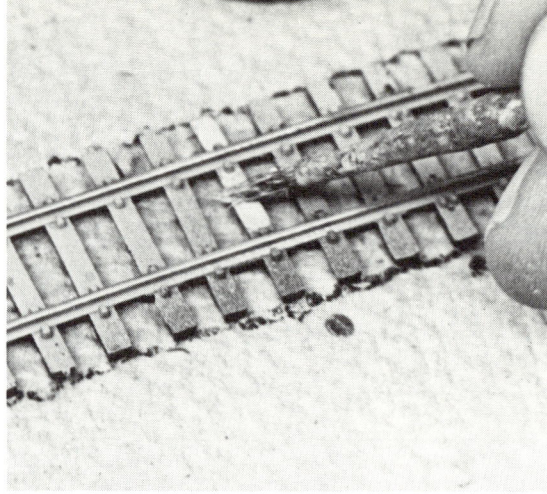

Fig. 9. Above left. Nothing makes the rail look more realistic more quickly than just painting it. **Above middle.** Malcolm eliminates the sameness of the ties by painting them with a variety of grays and earth colors. **Above right.** Cleaning the track goes quickly using a Bright Boy abrasive block.

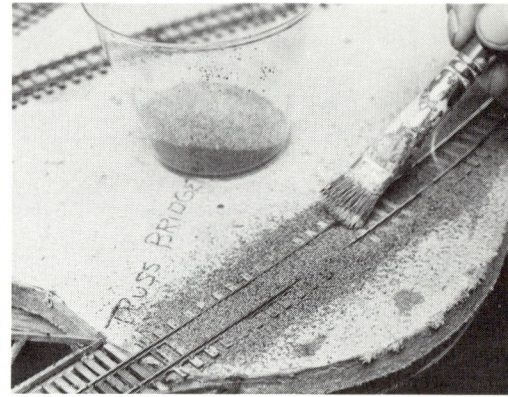

Fig. 10. Right. A disposable plastic glass makes a fine dispenser for ballast. **Middle right.** The ballast can be carefully shaped with a soft brush. After spraying on detergent-laced water until the ballast is soaked, details like old ties can be added. **Far right.** Diluted matte medium can be applied with an old glue bottle or a household sprayer.

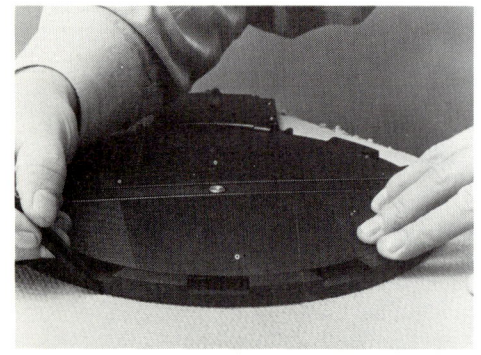
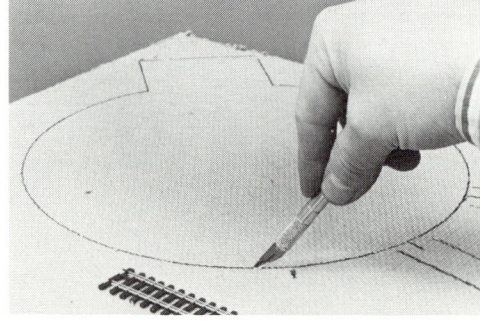
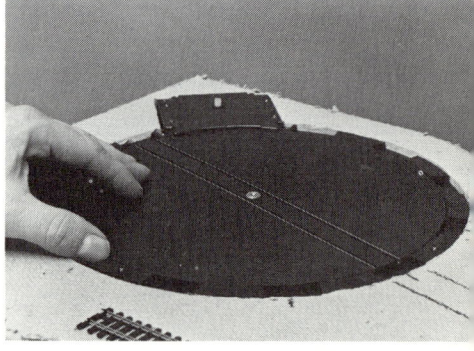
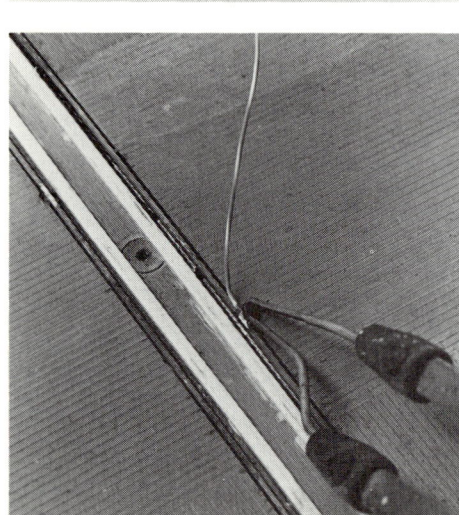
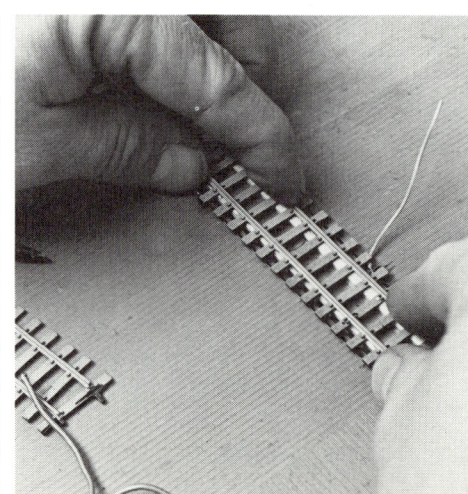

like to brush some with Floquil's Primer and others with Earth, Foundation, Maple, or Driftwood full strength right out of the bottle. Later on, if you feel that the track looks too stark, you can tone it down and blend it into the surrounding area with an airbrush loaded with Floquil Earth.

TRACK BALLASTING

Some modelers ballast track after they have spiked the last tie; others like to wait until the scenery is complete. On the SJC I did it both ways with equally good results.

On many western narrow gauge lines the ballast was little more than an afterthought, with more dirt thrown in than crushed rock. Weeds sprouted along the sides and often grew in the ballast itself. To represent such ballast I like to use real dirt sifted to the right consistency. A lot of commercial products are too uniform for a narrow gauge operation.

If you don't want to dig your own dirt, you can certainly buy it. One company that packages several shades of finely sifted dirt is the Rock Quarry. I like their Pink Sandstone Fine for representing crushed granite. I come back later and sprinkle on shades of gray and charcoal to simulate coal cinders, especially in the yard areas.

Before starting to ballast you can give the points and throwbar of a turnout a spray shot of WD-40 lubricant. This will help prevent the moving parts from becoming glued stuck, and you'll have an easier time getting the turnout to work well later.

To ballast track, begin by spreading a line of ballast along the middle of the ties between the rails, using a throw-away plastic or paper cup as a dispenser, as shown in fig. 10. Use a 1" brush to work the ballast in and around the ties, being careful not to get any particles in turnout points and switch motors. Level the ballast so the tops of the ties show on the main, but cover some ties in the yard areas and sidings. Don't worry about being too neat.

Take an atomizer bottle (I like to steal my wife's), fill it with tap water, and then add a few drops of liquid detergent. Spray the ballasted area of the track thoroughly. You want to see the water pooling up.

Next take diluted matte medium and water (⅔ water, ⅓ matte medium) and spread it along the wetted ballast. Now is a good time to add assorted details, such as old rotted ties and maybe a few rusty metal objects.

Let the area dry for a day, and then clean the rail tops with a Bright Boy abrasive pad. Finish up by scraping away unwanted particles of ballast from the inside rail surfaces with the blade of a small screwdriver.

THE TURNTABLE

To make the turntable at Montrose I started with an inexpensive plastic unit from Atlas and kitbashed it into a gallows-type table similar to the ones used by the Southern Pacific narrow gauge. You can motorize the turntable or control it manually. I turn mine with a hand crank located nearby.

Figure 11 shows how I recessed the turntable into the Homasote. Painting the unit, as shown in fig. 12, quickly removed it from the toy category.

As shown in fig. 13, I didn't try to remove the built-in standard gauge track. Rather, I just laid the 3-foot-gauge track on top of it and ran jumper wires from the HO track to the HOn3.

I pilfered the gallows from an old kit. Sequoia makes a structure you could use, or you could easily scratchbuild one. A little wood planking, as shown in fig. 14, completes the conversion.

Next we'll look at the magic of command control and install PSI's Dynatrol system on the layout. Meanwhile, if you're like me, you've probably already tacked on some test leads in a place or two and hooked up an old power pack, just so you can see a train run! ♦

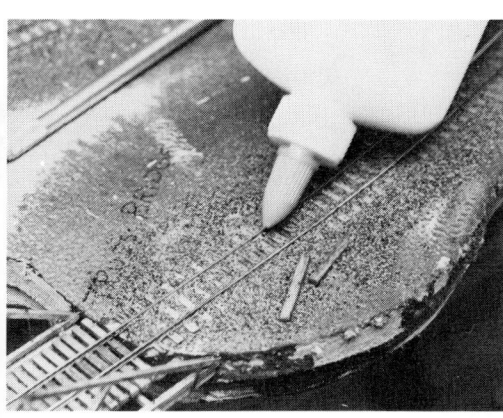

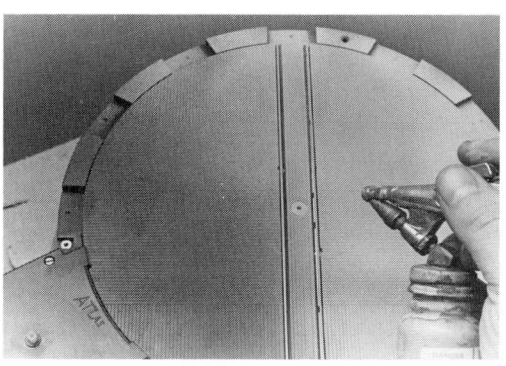

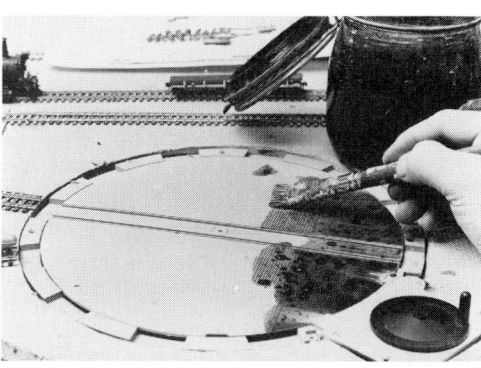

Fig. 11. Far left. The Montrose turntable started out as an inexpensive Atlas plastic model. Malcolm traced its outline on the Homasote with a felt-tip pen. **Middle left.** Using an X-acto knife he cut a hole in the Homasote so the unit could be screwed to the plywood base. **Left.** Positions for the two lead tracks have been carefully marked.

Fig. 12. Right. Malcolm airbrushed the table, using Floquil's Foundation. **Far right.** For that well-used look he stained it with a dilute solution of India ink. A drop of detergent helped the ink flow into the crevices.

Fig. 13. Far left. Malcolm soldered jumper wires to the bridge's standard gauge rails. Then he cemented wood strips next to the built-in rails, making sure they were even with the tops of the rails. **Middle left.** Next he cemented on a length of HOn3 flexible track. **Left.** After cementing on the gallows framework, he added cardboard shims to support the ends of the approach tracks.

Fig. 14. Right. Scribed balsa planking, supported by stripwood furring strips, hides modifications. To simulate oil stains Malcolm dabbed on Engine Black, then hit it with a brushload of thinner that made it spread and soak in. **Far right.** The depressions in the outer ring, intended to accept standard gauge approach tracks, were covered over with masking tape and later hidden when the scenery material was added.

John Romberger walks along with his train on the author's HOn3 San Juan Central. The railroad is equipped with command control.

SAN 4 JUAN CENTRAL

Wiring the San Juan Central

Using PSI's Dynatrol system makes this job much easier

ONE WORD can be used to describe the wiring of the San Juan Central: Easy! Forget the yards of tedious wire stringing, banks of toggle switches, and cockpit-like control panels associated with conventional block control — how about command control?

Imagine being able to operate two or more locomotives on the same stretch of track completely independent of each other. With command control you can. How about adding a helper to that heavy train starting up a 3 percent grade and being able to do it without having to bring everything to a halt? With command control it's no problem. And the same goes for dozens of other routine, multiengine train movements required to operate the railroad prototypically.

If I sound like I'm sold on command control, I am. Really, the most demanding job associated with installing my PSI Dynatrol system was mounting the receivers in the locomotives, and these could be handled on the TV tray while watching an episode of *Mr. Science* on cable TV.

And just what is command control? Well, the way the folks at PSI put it, "... Dynatrol operates by transmission of duty cycle modulated supersonic carrier control frequencies superimposed on the DC track voltage."

In other words, each locomotive has something like a radio receiver in it which is tuned to a specific but different frequency from the other locomotives on the layout. In a way it's like being able to play different radio stations at the same time, using different radio sets. You determine which locomotive will be controlled by inserting a channel plug, actually a precision-tuned resistor, into the cab control. For each receiver installed in your locomotives you have a corresponding plug. The receivers, each being tuned to a different channel, will respond only to the commands transmitted through the rail to them specifically.

PSI sells their Dynatrol equipment by mail and through dealers. For more information you can write to them at 56 Bellis Circle, Cambridge, MA 02140. They request you enclose a stamped, self-addressed, legal-sized envelope.

One drawback to command control is

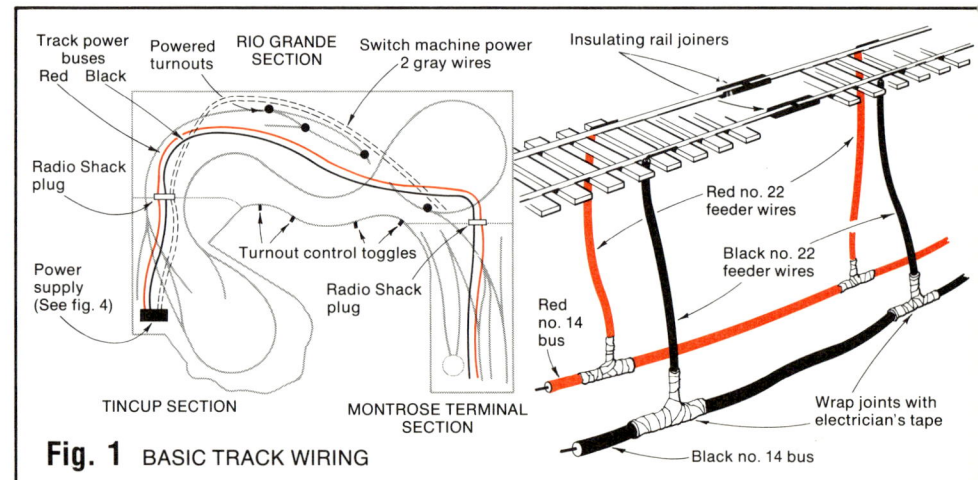

Fig. 1 BASIC TRACK WIRING

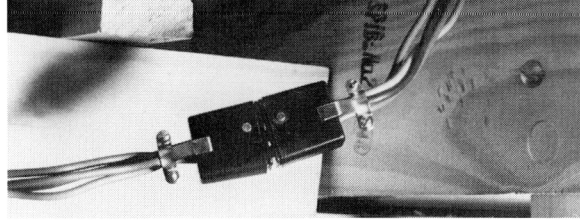

Fig. 2. Radio Shack plugs are used to connect the bus wires between the three sections, so it's easy to take the SJC apart.

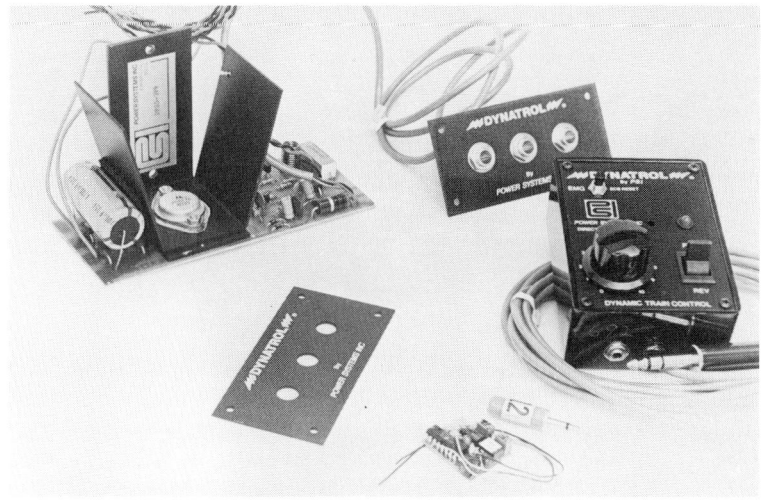

Fig. 3. These are the basic components of the PSI Dynatrol system. Upper left is the DPS5 power unit. The three jacks, upper right, come wired to the DPS5. Right is a walkaround controller. Just below it is a channel plug labeled 12. Any controller with this plug inserted will control any locomotive equipped with a channel 12 receiver. Below the plug is an RLL receiver. Left of the receiver is a faceplate for use with another trio of jacks.

Fig. 4 POWER SUPPLY

All the SJC power supply components are mounted to a plywood panel inside the Tincup section. Only 4 screws need be taken out to remove the Masonite panel hiding the components. The SJC has no control panels, and only a few control components appear on the profile boards

Labels (top figure):
- Radio Shack terminal strip (Optional)
- Radio Shack number 273 1505 transformer for switch machine power supply
- Signal 36-2 transformer for Dynatrol control system power
- 110V lighted SPST pushbutton for main power supply
- Plug jacks provided with Dynatrol DPS5
- Dynatrol DPS5 distribution power supply

Labels (bottom figure):
- Removable panel in profile board for access to plywood panel holding components
- 110V main power supply cord
- 110V lighted SPST pushbutton for main power supply
- Cab plugs (in jacks)
- Dynatrol Direct Function walkaround cabs
- Channel control plugs

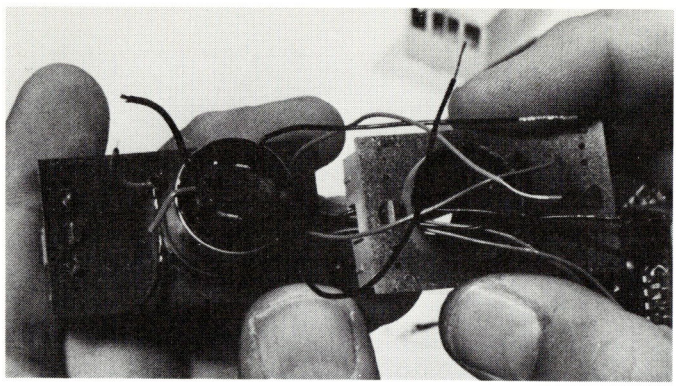 

Fig. 5. Above. Malcolm fitted Dynatrol's RSL receiver in his twin Grandt Line boxcabs. To make room in the receiver-carrying dummy, he sawed off the round motor housing. **Right.** The wires pass through the coupler pockets for a neat installation. Soldered wire joints are protected with shrink tubing.

its price. If the PSI or another system seems a bit rich for your model railroading tastes, you can easily wire the SJC for block control. John Olson explains how to do this in his book, BUILDING AN HO MODEL RAILROAD WITH PERSONALITY, and the subject is also covered in THE ABC's OF MODEL RAILROADING and Linn Westcott's HOW TO WIRE YOUR MODEL RAILROAD. All three books are published by Kalmbach Publishing Co.

GAPS AND FEEDERS

Simple as it may be, command control wiring involves more then just hooking two wires to the track and watching the trains roll. You still have to contend with the gap feeder rules I outlined in Chapter 3, but if you installed insulated joiners where they were indicated on the track plan, then you're all right.

The general scheme of wiring the SJC, as shown in fig. 1, was to run a pair of power bus wires (black for the inside, red for the outside rail) on the underside of the benchwork and to drop the track feeder wires to these buses.

As a general rule command control systems require heavier wiring than can be used with conventional systems. I used no. 14 wire for the buses and connected them between the portable sections with Radio Shack plugs, as shown in fig. 2. For the feeders to the rail I used no. 22 insulated stranded wire, also color coded black for the inside rail, red for the outside rail.

I tinned all the feeder wires before soldering them to the rail. Don't ever use an acid-core flux, even one labeled noncorrosive, for this type of soldering work.

To complete the solder joint I applied a little resin flux to the end of the tinned wire, held the wire to the rail, and applied heat with a 140-watt soldering gun, holding the gun to the rail, not to the wire. When the rail was hot enough, the solder from the tinned wire flowed to the rail, creating a neat, strong solder joint. Don't worry about melting the ties, just "get in and get out," as they say.

Before hooking a section's feeders to the buses I attached them to an old power pack to make sure a locomotive would run in the section. It's far easier to identify and correct an electrical problem at this stage than it would be once the wiring was finished.

Once under the layout with all those feeder wires dangling in front of me, it was a simple matter to strip the wire ends and connect the red feeders to the red bus and the black feeders to the black bus. All I had to do was strip a small section of insulation away from the bus using an X-acto knife, wrap the feeder around the bus, and solder.

THE POWER STATION

The basic elements of the Dynatrol system are shown in fig. 3. Figure 4 shows how I mounted the power components on a sheet of ¼" plywood fastened under the layout at Tincup. Installing the PSI power distribution station and transformer was easy, as the instructions that come with the PSI unit made it quite clear.

Warning: 110-volt house-current wiring can cause dangerous, even fatal, shocks and are a fire hazard if done improperly. If you're unsure of how to make 110-volt connections, get an expert to help you. Good manuals on 110-volt wiring are available at most hardware stores.

The transformer is not included in the PSI package, so you'll need to buy one. Try to get the recommended transformer made by Signal Transformer Co. An old toy transformer will also work, as long as the unit is rated at 18VAC and has sufficient power. PSI recommends 3 to 5 amps.

The wiring is simple. The green wires go to the power transformer, and the red and black wires go to the track. (See how cleverly that matches the color-coding on my track wiring!) Everything is covered in the PSI instructions, so be sure you consult them carefully before starting. [Editor's note: For maximum safety, all transformers should be mounted in metal cases that shield their leads.]

A RECEIVER FOR THE BOXCABS

The Grandt Line boxcabs, shown in fig. 5, are a good candidate for a quick, first installation. I use these little cuties for switching the yards at Montrose and Tincup. They're easy to assemble and they operate great.

The power drive is offered separately from the basic locomotive kit. You'll have about $50 tied up in a powered unit before you add the receiver, but to me this engine is a real bargain when it comes to narrow gauge motive power.

There wasn't room for a receiver in a single powered unit, so I decided to use two boxcabs coupled together. One cab carries the receiver; the other is motorized. It's possible to squeeze a PSI receiver into one of these cabs without modification, but it fits better if you cut off the motor collar molded into the bottom of the flooring. I used a razor saw for the job.

I drilled four holes in the floor of the dummy towards the end that faces the powered unit. The wires go out through the floor and the coupler pocket to the coupler pocket of the powered unit. From there they go through the powered unit's floor and are attached to the motor leads.

I used the plastic wheelsets that come with it for the dummy cab, but some of you may prefer metal wheels and a set of wipers to gain more electrical pickup. I've found that the two-wheel pickup gives pretty amazing performance.

One of the big advantages of a command control system is that you automatically have constant lighting. Because 13 volts are on the track at all times, the headlight will continue glowing even while the locomotive is standing still. I took advantage of this feature on the Grandt Line boxcabs by drilling out the plastic cast-on headlights and installing 16-volt bulbs. Dropping resistors (about 220 ohms) protect the bulbs.

You'll probably need to add weight to both boxcab interiors, just to help keep them on the track. Adding weight to the power unit also gives you more pulling power. A good method for adding weight is to visit your hobby shop and purchase a strip of model airplane weights with adhesive backing. Wrap those you use with tape to prevent the receiver from contacting a hard surface and help protect it from shock.

All of this might sound like a lot of tedious work, but it all came together for me in about an hour.

INSTALLING RECEIVERS IN ROUNDHOUSE STEAMERS

Figure 6 shows how I installed a small

PSI receiver in San Juan Central steamer no. 360. To make room for the receiver I had to remove the coal bunker by cutting it free along the inside seams. You can drill a few holes or use a heated knife to form a slot to get a razor saw started. Discard this portion of the tender. You'll have to fabricate a new coal bunker and hide the receiver beneath a high coal load.

Once the receiver fit, I secured it with double-faced foam tape. Next I drilled three small holes in the coal door and ran three wires through these holes to the engine. One of the black (fourth) wires attaches to the tender frame, the other to one lead coming from the headlight. Both gray wires attach to the motor leads. The other headlight wire is soldered to a 220-ohm resistor and attaches to the frame.

One last suggestion — insulate your splices with heat-shrink tubing. I used U. S. Modeltronics no. 3010.

TURNOUTS AND SWITCH MACHINES

Most of the turnouts on the SJC are thrown by Caboose Hobbies hand throws, but in those hard-to-reach places on the Rio Grande section I used Point Drives by Mann-Made Products, as shown in fig. 7. These move the switch points by means of a jack screw driven by an electric motor that operates on 6- to 12-volt AC or DC power. Mine are powered by their own 6-volt AC transformer, shown in fig. 4.

I mounted the Point Drive machines under the benchwork and used Anderson links for a mechanical connection to the points. See fig. 6. A single length of piano wire is all that's needed to make the mechanical link between the switch machine and the Anderson linkage. I recommend doing as much of the hookup work as you can at the workbench. You can connect most of the wires and do most of the soldering before crawling under the layout.

To hook up the switch machines I used yellow wire that couldn't be confused with the red and black used for the control wiring.

CONTROL PANELS

The SJC's control panels are a snap, basically because there aren't any! We don't need the traditional (and usually complicated) control panel with its array of buttons and switches. The few controls we have for the layout are arranged simply on the profile boards to complement our walkaround feature. The single-pole, double-throw toggle to throw a particular turnout is on the profile board directly in front of it — you reach for the correct control instinctively.

Incidentally, I find it better to have the toggle switches move vertically instead of horizontally, since this protects them from being thrown by a wayward body moving through the aisleway. For futher protection and even neater appearance, you could recess the toggles and other controls.

So much for the wiring. Like I said, it's easy. Next we'll turn to scenery and making mountains out of foam. I think anyone wanting to build a lightweight portable layout or module will find the techniques interesting. ○

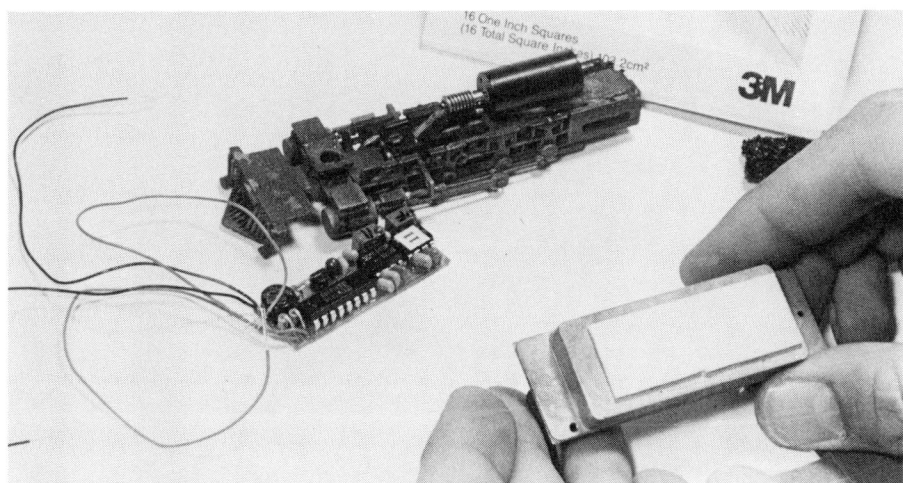

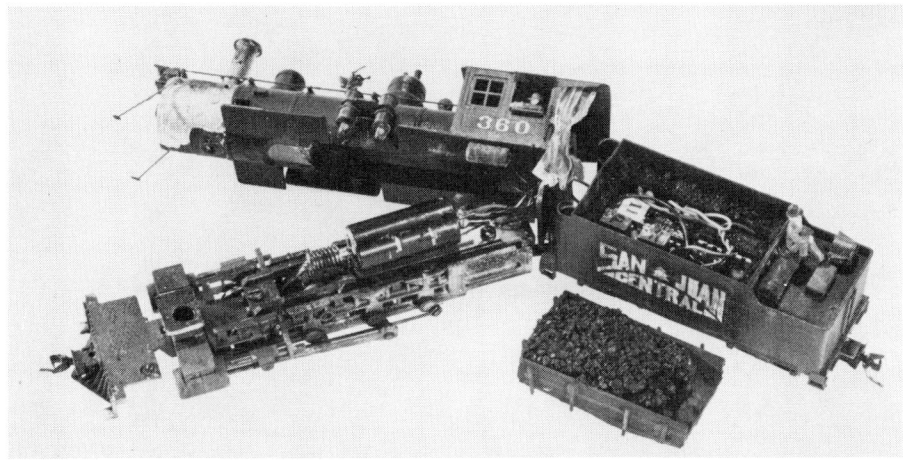

Fig. 6. Top. Double-sided foam tape makes it easy to mount the Dynatrol RLL receiver to the Roundhouse tender floor. **Above.** After installation the receiver is hidden under extended coal bunker sides.

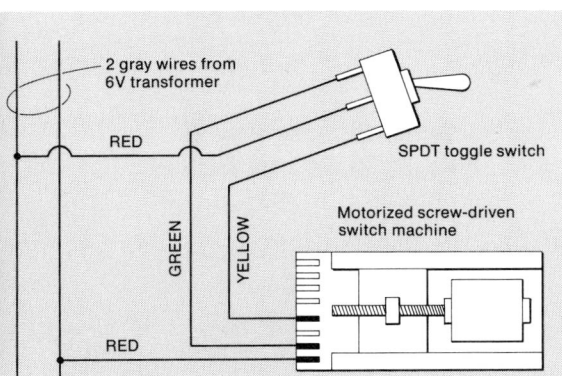 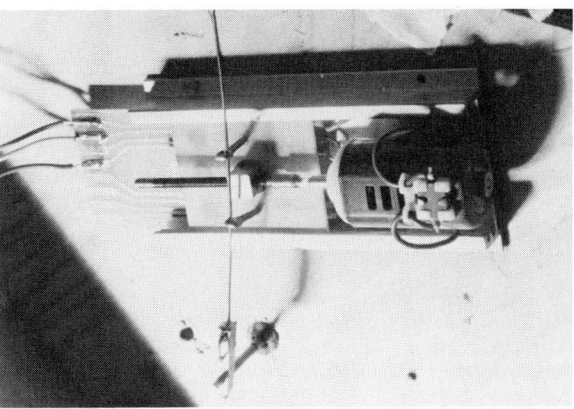 

Fig. 7. Left and center. Hard-to-reach turnouts on the Rio Grande section are thrown by Mann-Made Point Drive switch machines and Anderson turnout links mounted under the layout. **Right.** The switch machines are controlled by simple toggle switches mounted on the sides of the layout.

Malcolm makes soaring pine trees like those on the right from balsa trunks and caspia branches. The dying tree, left, is made the same way, but with most of the flowers removed from the caspia branches.

Scenery for the San Juan Central

Those acres of rock are foam castings and weigh practically nothing

SCENERY — now we've come to that part of layout building where we breathe life into our creation. Scenery is also the most personal aspect of model railroading. Good trackwork will look about the same, regardless of who does it, but scenery can't help reflecting that personal touch. As the legendary John Allen, builder of the beautiful Gorre & Daphetid, once said, scenery isn't just something to keep the trains from falling to the floor! Visitors see the scenery first, and if it's not pleasing they may not look beyond it.

Obviously, scenery is an area where we can make the San Juan Central really stand out. After all, southwestern Colorado offers almost every type of dramatic scenery imaginable, except oceans and swamps.

The scenery I've designed for the SJC

The dramatic rock faces on the HOn3 San Juan Central are made from polyfoam. They weigh practically nothing and are virtually damage-proof.

reflects the way I like scenery to look. Feel free to express yourself differently. You can use my ideas merely as a springboard towards building a layout that is more your own. In fact, you could use just the track plan and build a railroad that had nothing to do with Colorado at all.

As the photos often show, I built much of the scenery even before all the track was laid. I don't like to do just one thing for long, and scenery construction can be a welcome relief, freeing you from jobs that are more technically demanding. After all, this is a hobby, so why not do what you want to when you feel like it.

FOAM CONSTRUCTION

To keep the layout light but strong, I used rigid foam for my scenic forms. Foam is easy to work and cleans up with a vacuum cleaner. You aren't racing the clock as you do with plaster, so you can work slower and more carefully. You can even build large sections at the workbench and attach them to the layout later.

Of course, you don't have to use foam at all on your version of the SJC. A very popular and extremely effective way of building scenery is the plaster hardshell method. John Olson used this technique on his standard gauge Jerome & Southwestern, and it's detailed in his book on that layout, BUILDING AN HO MODEL RAILROAD WITH PERSONALITY.

I've used hardshell for my home layout, the Denver & Rio Chama Western, and recommend it highly for *permanent* layouts. A portable layout is quite another matter though. Plaster is heavy and brittle, two qualities you definitely don't want on a layout designed to be moved. Give foam scenery a pretty good shot with a hammer and you may dent it a little, but you won't break it.

The SJC's Grandt Line boxcabs limber up for morning switching duties. Malcolm models water with two-part epoxy. Looks like the flatcar hasn't been in the river long and is worth retrieving.

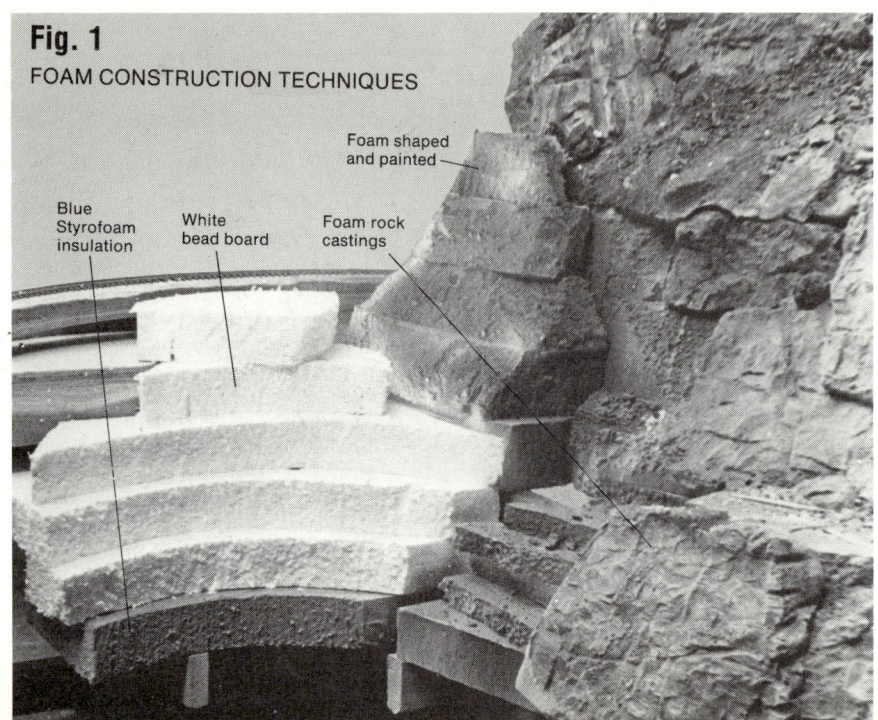

Fig. 1 FOAM CONSTRUCTION TECHNIQUES

Blue Styrofoam insulation — White bead board — Foam rock castings — Foam shaped and painted

Fig. 2. Foam can be shaped quickly with any cutting tool. Neatness is not critical, as the rock castings and ground cover will hide the base.

I used two basic types of foam for the scenery sub-base, as shown in fig. 1. Where there was a solid foundation I used white bead board of the kind often used in packaging. In areas where more firm support was called for, I used extruded Styrofoam. You can buy both bead board and extruded Styrofoam at lumberyards and building supply stores. The white bead board usually comes in 1"-thick 2 x 6-foot sheets sold 10 to a package. Dow Corning's extruded Styrofoam is blue and comes in 2 x 8-foot sheets with thicknesses of ¾", 1", 1½", 2", 2½", and 3".

I built up the scenery forms in layers, something like a wedding cake. A power saber saw or a keyhole saw make short work of cutting the foam. See fig. 2. A latex contact cement is good for gluing the layers together, but I used Mastic no. 11, a product marketed by Dow Corning especially for gluing Styrofoam.

You can pin the stacked sections together with nails to hold them until the glue dries. File the forms to final shape with a rasp or a knife. Keep the vacuum cleaner handy — that foam dust wants to get everywhere! And don't wear a wool sweater while working with foam or you'll come out looking like the sheep the wool came from.

Building up the various forms takes some seat-of-the-pants engineering. The photos in fig. 3 show ways I solved various scenery problems as I came to them.

You can use textured paint or Sculptamold to fill cracks and other unwanted holes in the Styrofoam. Sculptamold is a plaster-like product sold at art supply stores. It's lightweight but extremely tough, and you can apply it easily with a pallet knife.

FOAM ROCKS

When you're talking Colorado Rockies you're talking lots of rocks, and as far as I'm concerned the best way to make lots of rocks quickly is to cast them in rubber

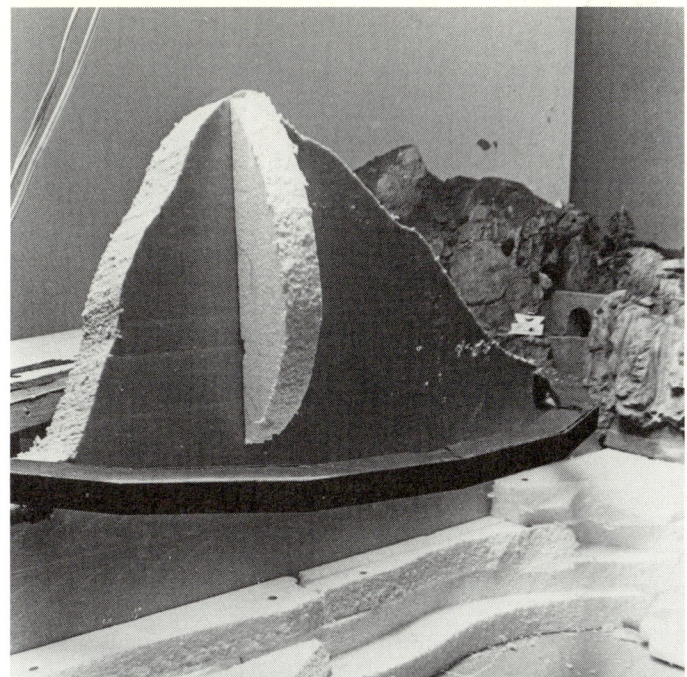

Fig. 3. Building up basic forms from sheet foam required some creative engineering. **Left.** Malcolm made the large pinnacle rock at Montrose by first making this rough bead-board core, then adding foam rock castings. **Above left.** For its extra strength extruded Styrofoam was used for the riverbed at Crazy Horse Bridge. The larger vertical form for the mountain is also blue Styrofoam. The remaining foam is less strong but less expensive white bead board, glued together and pinned with nails. **Above.** At the rear of the layout masking tape was sufficient to tie the foam panels together until the polyfoam rocks could be wet-mounted and bind the assembly solidly.

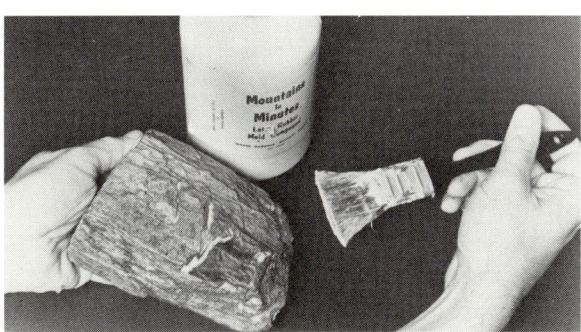
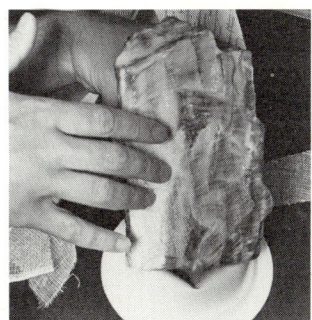

Fig. 4. Far left. Malcolm makes his own rock molds by brushing liquid latex rubber onto suitable masters, such as real rocks or chunks of coal. Here he's using a piece of petrified wood. **Left.** After painting on three or four coats of rubber, allowing each coat to dry, Malcolm adds a layer of surgical gauze for reinforcement, then finishes the job with two more coats of rubber.

molds. You can buy rock molds (rocks too for that matter) at your hobby shop, or you can make your own, as shown in fig. 4. The latex will capture fine strata and details, giving you a mold that's ready to duplicate the intricate works of Mother Nature. Most of us will get far quicker and better results with castings than we would carving rocks by hand.

For the sake of lightness and durability, I cast my rocks with expandable polyurethane, although plaster would be a better choice on a permanent layout because it reproduces fine detail better. If you also choose to go the lightweight route, I recommend you purchase the Mountains in Minutes starter kit from ISLE Laboratories. It comes with a very complete set of instructions.

The Mountains in Minutes polyfoam consists of two parts, a resin and a catalyst, that can be mixed in a disposable paper cup and poured into a latex mold. A chemical reaction causes the polyfoam to expand greatly, so it takes a little practice to learn how much mixture to pour.

As shown in fig. 5, use *plenty* of mold release and allow it to dry thoroughly before pouring in the chemicals. Otherwise the polyfoam will adhere to the mold and become a useless mess, *and* you'll have lost a good mold.

One good mold-release agent readily available is Armor-All, sold in most auto

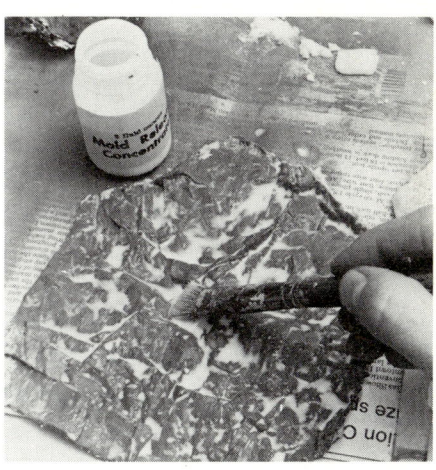

Fig. 5. A vital step in making polyfoam rock castings is swabbing on several coats of mold release.

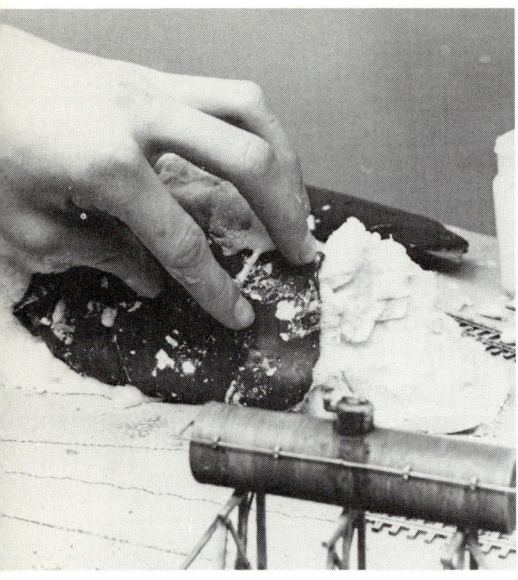

Fig. 6. Malcolm uses two basic methods for applying foam castings to the layout. **Above.** They can be easily wet-mounted to a firm foam base. **Right.** Castings can also be permitted to dry in the mold, then glued in place and held with pins until the white glue sets.

parts stores. Normally it's used for reconditioning vinyl car tops, but because it contains liquid silicone, we can use it as a release agent in molds.

As shown in fig. 6, you can press the mold against the scenery base before the foam has set and wet mount the casting, or you can let it harden in the mold and then glue it on the layout. With the latter technique you can sometimes get by with no support at all or only a little masking tape or cardboard.

Figure 7 shows a way I discovered for making interesting rock pinnacles by placing foam in a flat mold, waiting for it to begin expanding, then rolling it up, taping it closed, and letting it harden. It looks weird but works great.

Other types of polyfoam can be used to create lightweight rocks. The spray-can type used for insulation around windows and doors will work. An example is shown in fig. 8. You can purchase spray foam at some hardware stores or at variety stores like Target or K Mart. The spray foam doesn't really come out of the can in a spray; it's more like shaving cream and sort of foams out.

Probably the most economical way to purchase polyurethane is from a dealer in plastics. I purchased a gallon kit (consisting of resin and catalyst) from a plastics dealer in Dallas for $59. Believe me, a gallon goes a long way.

COLORING FOAM ROCKS

After the castings are hard I spray them with a base coat of Pactra Light Earth, as shown in fig. 9. I make sure to apply it lightly, as a heavy coat will attack the polyfoam. Another good method would be to brush on a coat of thinned tan latex paint.

After the base coat has dried, I drybrush the rocks with earth tones of acrylic artist's paints straight from the tube. Red oxide, burnt sienna, and a little yellow ochre are good. I'm careful not to overdo it, just putting on a little dab here and there. Before the acrylic dries, I hit the rock full force with water from an atomizer bottle. This causes the colors to penetrate the strata, cracks, and crevices without overrunning and neutralizing each other. You can speed the drying of these colors with a hair dryer.

Next, I apply a wash of India ink diluted with water, making the solution just strong enough to accent the cracks and crevices. The India ink treatment makes the rock appear somewhat dark, but you can lighten the rock face a bit by drybrushing it with acrylic white after the ink has dried.

Some of the castings may have fine holes caused by tiny air bubbles. A few such holes are no problem, but if there are too many or they are too big, you can touch them up with a tube of acrylic putty of the sort sold for touching up nail holes in paneling. Use a color that matches the Pactra Light Earth. Squirt a little out on the end of your finger and press it into the holes. You can sand it later and touch up the area with paint.

Really bad castings can be salvaged with thinned texture paint. Brush on the paint, then wipe it off with a cloth.

Figure 10 shows some of my techniques for installing foam retaining walls. You'll generally want to dry-mount these, as they should have relatively flat surfaces.

GROUND COVER

Before adding any texturing materials I painted the Styrofoam ground with spray paint. Again, I used Pactra's Light Earth in a spray can. Thinned latex paint could also be used.

I used all natural earth materials for ground cover on the SJC, beginning with decomposed granite which I applied over practically everything. If you can't find decomposed granite in your area, clay-type cat-box filler can be substituted.

The Rock Quarry markets a large line of natural dirt materials sold in hobby shops. A neat thing about using their products is that all the sifting has been done for you. Many colors and textures are available.

I like to dust on various shades of fine dirt first, then add a little of the coarser material, as shown in fig. 11. Larger rocks go along the bottoms of hillsides where they would end up after cascading down from mountain faces.

Using a spray bottle I saturate the dirt-covered area with detergent-laced water. Then I apply a white glue and water mixture (⅔ water, ⅓ glue with a couple of drops of detergent tossed in as a wetting agent), soaking the area completely. An old glue bottle, as shown in fig. 11, or something like a plastic mustard dispenser makes a good glue applicator. While the area is still wet I add weeds, discarded boards, and other details, such as drain pipes made from soda straws. The one shown in fig. 11 is a souvenir of the Golden Arches, but Burger King's would probably work too.

GRASS AND WEEDS

I used Woodland Scenics ground foam

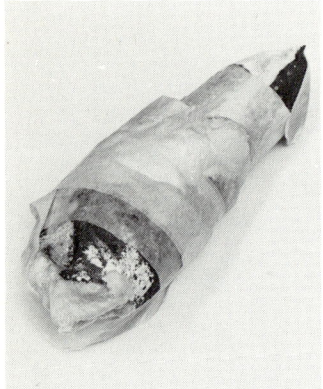

Fig. 7. Left. Malcolm made a distinctive pinnacle rock by loading a flat rubber mold with polyfoam, waiting until the foam began to set, then rolling the mold up and taping it with masking tape. **Right.** He carved a seat for the formation in the hillside, then cemented the rock to the hill with white glue.

Fig. 8. Spray-can foam insulation can also be used for foam rocks. The method is neat but fairly expensive.

Fig. 9. Above. The first step in painting foam rocks and ground is spraying on Pactra's Light Earth. Malcolm adds color by brushing on acrylics then spraying them with water to blend them. Dilute India ink darkens cracks and crevices. **Right.** Detail is brought out by drybrushing with white acrylic straight from the tube.

Fig. 10. Left. Foam retaining walls are best dry-mounted. Here Malcolm marks off a section for a bridge abutment. **Center.** Once cemented in place the wall is painted the same as rocks would be. **Right.** Spackling compound worked in with a stiff brush hides a joint between wall sections.

Fig. 11. Above. Malcolm details the ground with real dirt and rocks. **Right.** He uses a spray bottle to thoroughly wet scenery materials, then bonds them with diluted white glue. **Far right.** Details like culverts are worked into the wet ground.

Fig. 12. Stripwood planks, distressed and weathered, make nice grade crossings. Malcolm is wetting the area prior to adding diluted white glue.

for grass, alternating the shades between their Earth and Blended Turf to give a highlighted effect to the slopes.

For taller grass I like Boyd's Electrostatic grass. An effective way of using this product is to first hit an area with spray adhesive, then use the Boyd Models plastic applicator to shoot the flocking onto the glue-covered scene. Squeezing the applicator in short bursts forces the flocking (grass) out sharply. Most of the blades fly through the air and stick standing up to create a beautiful grassy effect. As applied, the flocking is a bit too bright, but it can be toned down with a light airbrushing of Floquil's Foundation or Earth.

Notice we are adding texture upon texture to create density and variety. To further texture some areas I added bits and clumps of lichen for a more lush effect. These had been sprayed with adhesive and dusted with various shades of ground foam. I dab the foam-covered lichen with white glue and attach it to the layout, sometimes using a toothpick to pin it to the foam until the glue dries.

For an added bit of color you can sprinkle on some brightly colored foam in shades of red, yellow, and white to represent flowers. Go easy! It takes only a little bit to be convincing.

ROADS

To model roads I first make a foam base, either carving it from rigid foam or building it up with polyfoam. I paint it an earth color then dust it lightly with finely sifted, lightly colored sand and dirt. Then I bond it just as I do ground cover, being careful not to wash away the dirt.

Once the road is thoroughly wet, I carve in ruts with a dental pick by drawing (almost dragging) the point lightly along the roadway. After the road has dried I knock any excess dirt from the ruts and vacuum it up. I drybrush the road with a light tan color (a mixture of Floquil Earth and Reefer White) to highlight the tops of the ruts, leaving the potholes and deeper ruts a darker color.

Weeds can be added sparingly along the edges of the road and down the middle to simulate a lack of traffic. This helps to create that "back in the sticks" look.

As shown in fig. 12, I make road crossings by laying scale 1 x 6s or 1 x 8s on the ties. A quick run-through with a set of trucks is good for checking clearances, then I work sifted dirt up to the planks. I use a drafting pen and India ink to poke in small holes to represent nails.

CASPIA PINE TREES

Many modelers seem to believe that western scenery is devoid of green stuff, but let me assure you there are trees aplenty in the canyons and parks of southwestern Colorado, and plenty of other vegetation, too.

Pine and aspen dot the landscape in great numbers, and modeling autumn will give us a chance to capture that time of year when the burnt orange and yellow leaves of the aspen give the high-country slopes a bonanza of color. Of course, the pine trees are green all year, and pine is the type of tree seen most often in the area we're modeling.

For me, the most convincing pine tree is one made by adding caspia branches to a tapered balsa trunk, as shown in fig. 13. Caspia is sold in florist shops. Your hobby dealer should have the balsa you need for the trunks — ¼"-square balsa is good for most pines; you might want some ½" square for the really big babies.

I carve my trunks with a wood rasp and use a wire brush to stroke some texture into them. To stain the trunks I use my solution of diluted India ink again to achieve a silvery gray appearance with a tinge of brown. A-West's Weather-It is also good for this. Thin washes of red oxide and light yellow are good for simulating redwoods or ponderosa pines.

I drill or press random holes in the trunks then dip individual caspia stems in white glue and insert them, using shorter lengths towards the top of the trunk and longer ones lower down.

Next I hit the branches with green spray paint, being careful to aim off center so as not to hit the trunk. One color I like is Pactra's Forest Green.

After spraying the colored branches with 3M adhesive, I dust on some green ground foam, dropping it on from above like snow. A little experimentation will determine the best adhesive-to-foam ratio. You can add dead limbs by using caspia without the flowers.

For planting purposes I stick toothpicks in the bottoms of the trunks. With foam scenery you can just poke the trees into position.

CASPIA ASPEN TREES

Aspen trees can also be made from caspia. Paint some caspia stems white to represent trunks, then touch the trunk and limbs here and there with black to simulate the markings of real aspens. Acrylic fiber, the kind used for pillow stuffing, is good for supporting the foliage. Stretch the fiber and fluff it out over the branches so it is almost transparent. Give it a shot of 3M spray adhesive then dust on yellow ground foam very lightly. Don't use too much foam,

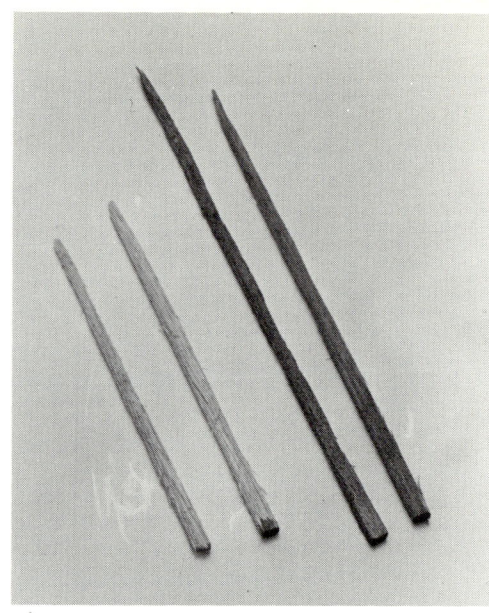

Fig. 13. Above. To make caspia pine trees Malcolm first made balsa trunks. **Right.** Then he inserted the caspia branches. **Next right.** He sprayed the branches green. **Far right.** Last came spraying the branches with an adhesive and sprinkling on a bit of ground foam.

as you are going for that lacy, see-through look.

Plant your trees in groupings of three or more. Don't ask me why, but trees never seem to look right planted in pairs. Detail the area with a few dead limbs lying about.

You can make deciduous trees other than aspens using the same technique. Leave the caspia trunks their natural color or spray them light brown. Use green foam instead of yellow. Once the first sprinkling of foam has set, spray on more adhesive and dust on a lighter shade of green. This will give the effect of a tree seen in sunlight, with the leaves in shadow appearing dark and those receiving more light popping out.

Woodland Scenics offers deciduous tree kits with soft metal trunks and limbs which can be bent to a variety of shapes and detailed with paint. The kit comes with foam already attached to fiber and

Fig. 14. Far left. To give it strength the riverbed at Crazy Horse bridge was made from 2" extruded Styrofoam. Here Malcolm is preparing to build the near bank. **Left.** The riverbed was detailed with rocks, dirt, and other details. **Above.** Malcolm poured a two-part epoxy into the stream bed. **Right.** Once the epoxy had begun to set up, Malcolm used a scribing tool to work in some swirling water.

ready for application to the trunks. You can use these trees with their extra trunk detail up front on the layout and work the caspia stem trees in behind.

Sprigs of caspia right out of the bundle can be used here and there as an effective contrast to the green foliage. Leave the flowers on.

MODELING WATER

The Colorado narrow gauge followed twisting mountain streams and rivers into gold and silver country, riding the shelves of granite carved out by white water rivers such as the Animas, Clear Creek, and Gunnison. I love to model these white-water streams.

Figure 14 shows how I modeled the Rio San Juan. I sprayed the foam riverbed with Pactra Light Earth, then prepared it using the same techniques I use for adding ground cover. I added logs, old tires, and rotted timbers. You could also add a wrecked auto or a boxcar that has tumbled into the stream, the result of a washout or a smash-up. As before, I wet everything thoroughly, then bonded it with diluted white glue.

It's important to let the riverbed dry thoroughly before adding the water, in this case an epoxy resin. I used Everfix brand because it is compatible with Styrofoam — says so right on the label. Before mixing up a batch of epoxy, I checked to make sure the riverbed was sealed. Epoxy will find the smallest possible hole and leak through.

I mixed the epoxy according to the manufacturer's directions, then added 20 percent more hardener. Also, I added a little color to the water by spraying just a dash of Pactra Forest Green into the mixture and stirring vigorously to create that translucent greenish murk. If you want blue-green add some Pactra Sky Blue along with the green.

I poured the mixture about 1/4"-thick into the riverbed and waited. After an hour it began to jell, and I picked at it with a sharp, pointed instrument to create those white-water swirls. You can use a hairdryer to speed the curing process, but be careful not to get the heat too close to the epoxy — it's possible to scorch it.

Once the epoxy had set I drybrushed on some white acrylic to highlight the tops of the rapids. Then I mixed up one more coat of epoxy, this time leaving out the color, and poured a thin layer over the hardened epoxy river to restore a uniform high gloss.

Well, we've covered a lot of ground in this chapter — that's a joke, son. It's high time for some HO civilization to move into our corner of the San Juan country, so next we'll take a look at how to build structures for the San Juan Central. ⛊

The McClanahan mine spur is built in a cut right in the Prairie Fire Inn's backyard. As this photo shows, the backs of buildings can be just as interesting as the fronts.

SAN 6 JUAN CENTRAL

Structures for the San Juan Central

Making small, colorful buildings that allow the scenery to dominate

IF YOU'VE ever taken a stroll down the main street of Victor, Black Hawk, or Cripple Creek, then you know the charm of those quaint false-front stores and gaudy hotels from Colorado's past. That's the feeling I wanted on the HO San Juan Central, and I set out to achieve it almost entirely with standard, off-the-shelf structure kits. Figure 1 lists the kits I used. I built most of them stock, although I did indulge in a tad of kitbashing in a few places here and there.

Most of these buildings aren't highly detailed, but once they've been weathered and placed in a scene complete with clutter, signs, people, trees, weeds, and vehicles, they come alive and help complete our narrow gauge illusion. And that's what the SJC is all about, creating a believable illusion.

I wanted an orchestrated balance between the scenery and the structures. Up close the buildings should be detailed and interesting, but from a distance I wanted them to blend into the scenery and be dominated by it. I wanted the buildings to be splashes of color and nostalgia — small and quaint "supporting players" to the trains.

Woodland Scenics and Magnuson offer some tiny buildings loaded with character, and you'll notice that I used several of these several times over. Four Wood-

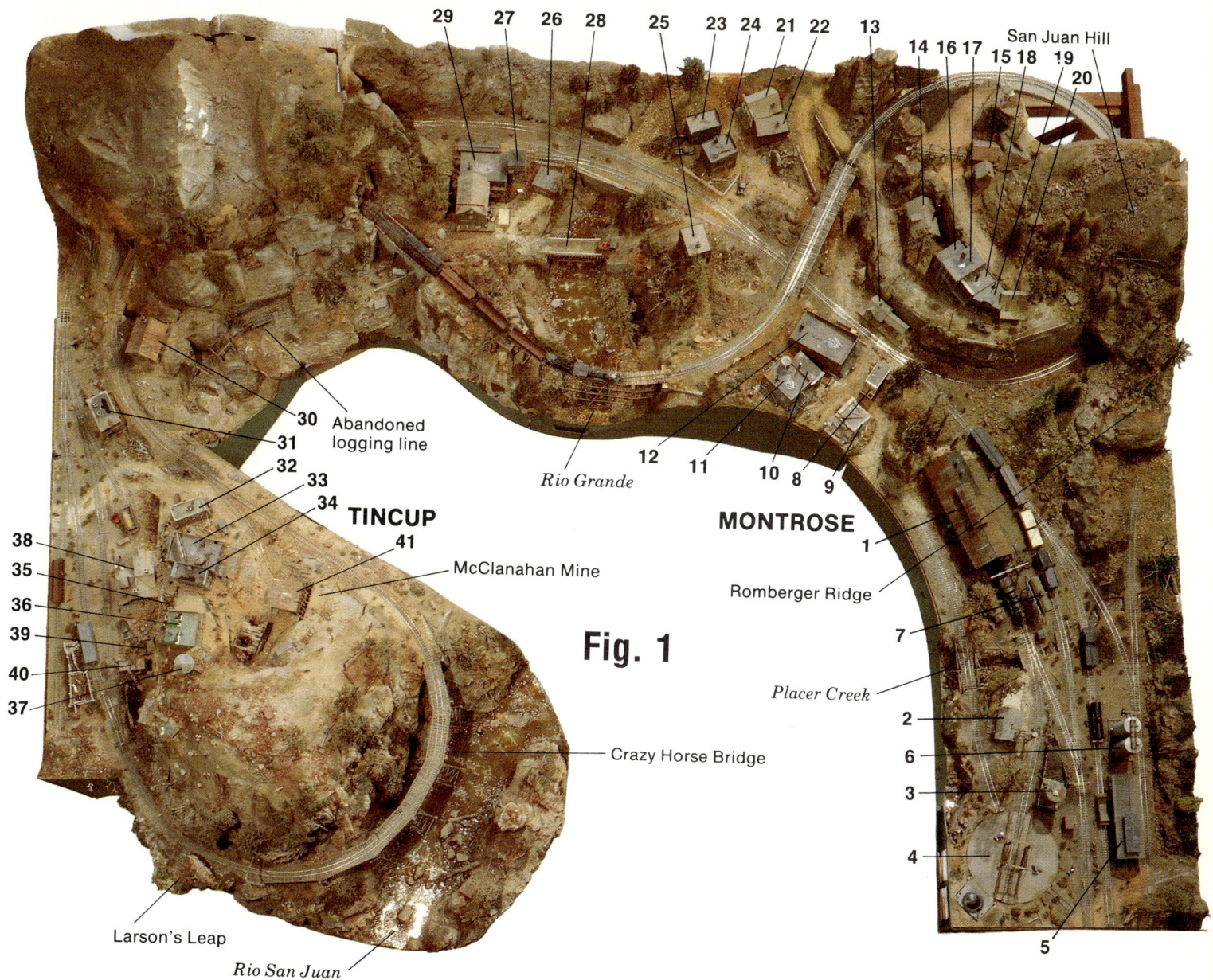

Fig. 1

STRUCTURES FOR THE SAN JUAN CENTRAL

1. Campbell no. 389 enginehouse
2. Tyco no. 7763 sandhouse
3. Tyco no. 7738 water tower. See fig. 6
4. Atlas no. 302 turntable. See February issue
5. Heljan no. 1766 freighthouse. Skylight replaced
6. Campbell no. 410 loading tanks
7. Model Die Casting no. 3361 tank car on scratchbuilt wood bents
8. Woodland Scenics no. 221 pharmacy
9. Thomas A. Yorke Sonora shop
10. Heljan no. 902 two small stores
11. Magnuson no. 537 practice kit store
12. Heljan no. 902 two small stores
13. Woodland Scenics no. 239 flag depot
14. Tyco no. 7778 hardware store
15. Scratchbuilt mine
16. Woodland Scenics no. 221 pharmacy. Converted to hotel
17. Magnuson no. 502 Miner's Union Hall. Left half only used
18. Magnuson no. 537 practice kit store
19. Magnuson no. 507 Bank of Victoria Falls. Upper two stories removed
20. Chooch no. 9004 Columbia depot. Kitbashed into gas station
21. Campbell no. 434 tobacco shop
22. AHM no. 15502 general store and billiards parlor. Converted to store
23. AHM no. 15501 ice cream parlor/boarding house. Converted to store
24. AHM no. 15502 store and billiards parlor. Converted to store
25. AHM no. 15501 ice cream parlor/boarding house. Converted to store
26. Tyco no. 7787 hotel (garage)
27. AHM no. 15706 water tower on lower part of NJ International no. 1971 water tower
28. Campbell no. 762 bridge. Inverted
29. O'Burn Millworks. See fig. 10
30. Scratchbuilt jail
31. Scratchbuilt hotel
32. Magnuson no. 537 practice store. Converted to Hayden's Hideaway
33. Tyco no. 7787 railroad hotel. Converted to Prairie Fire Inn
34. Woodland Scenics no. 221 pharmacy. Converted to rooming house
35. Scratchbuilt mining tower
36. Model Power no. 402 Wells Fargo Office. Converted to Lodge hall
37. NJ International no. 1971 water tower. Shortened
38. Tyco no. 7783 Rico station. Modified
39. AHM no. 15706 pumping station. Converted to windmill
40. MDC tender on base from AHM no. 15706 tank
41. Campbell no. 438 ore bin. Converted to McClanahan mine

Fig. 2. Above. So the scenery would dominate the towns, Malcolm used many small buildings and spaced them close together. Here's downtown Montrose.

Fig. 3. Right. Placing structures on various levels adds drama and keeps the eye moving in a scene, a principle clearly demonstrated in this shot of Tincup.

land Scenics pharmacies, for example, found a home on the SJC, but since they're all painted differently with the details changed here and there, most viewers never catch on.

Not only did I keep the buildings small, I also grouped them closely together. Compression of the sort shown in fig. 2 helps make the layout look larger than it really is. Taking advantage of the vertical dimension was also important. Placing the structures at different heights and working in retaining walls and winding roads all helped to create scenes that are exciting to look at and that keep the eyes moving from side to side as well as up and down. See figs. 2 and 3.

You might try to duplicate my efforts, building by building, wall by wall, or you might select those elements you like best and blend them with ideas of your own. These are the ideas and methods that worked for me. I'm glad to share them with you, and I hope you'll take it beyond what I've done here.

TIPS ON PLASTIC BUILDINGS

Many of the kits used on the SJC are of the inexpensive plastic variety. Assembled straight out of the box these tend to be a bit too pristine for our rowdy mountain communities. Keep in mind, though, that you can texture and distress plastic using the same techniques and tools you use when working

Fig. 4. To simulate mortar lines in plastic brick walls, Malcolm brushes on thinned Polly-S paint, lets it set up, then lightly wipes off the excess.

Fig. 5. Pastel chalk dust is excellent for weathering structures. Once the effects are satisfactory the dust can be fixed with a clear, flat overspray.

with wood. A razor-saw blade is good for working in some deep grain lines. For the look of weathered wood, first texture the plastic, then paint it with Floquil Foundation. After the paint dries stain the piece with India ink and alcohol.

That shine so characteristic of raw plastic really destroys realism, so usually we paint plastic models with flat model paints. I prefer to spray the paint on plastic, using an airbrush or aerosol can. Lacquer-base paints like Floquil will craze plastic surfaces if applied too heavily, so I'm careful to spray them on lightly and evenly. The paint should be almost dry when it hits the model. If you'd prefer to brush on Floquil, then coat the plastic surface with Floquil Barrier before you actually begin painting.

If you use an airbrush here's a helpful hint. Thin the stock paint 50/50 with Diosol (Floquil's thinner), stir the mixture well, then strain it through a piece of nylon hose to get rid of any tiny lumps.

Figure 4 shows my technique for finishing brick walls. I like Floquil's Tuscan Red as a basic brick color, although you certainly wouldn't want to use the same color on all of your brick buildings. Other reds, yellows, and earth tones are also good. I spray on an even coat and let it dry for a couple of hours.

Polly-S is good for mortar lines. It's also made by Floquil but is a water-base paint and won't disturb the base coat. I thin a capful of Polly-S White with wa-

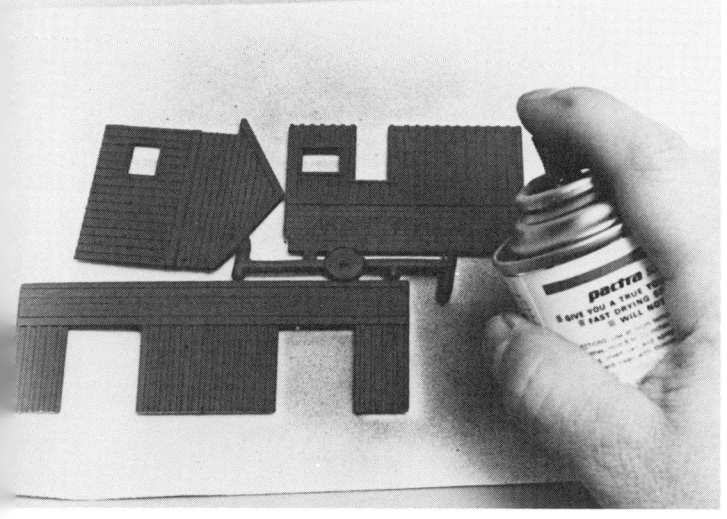  

Fig. 6. Left. To simulate peeling paint the author first dabs rubber cement onto a gray surface. **Above.** Next he sprays on the color coat. **Right.** After the color has dried an hour he uses a pencil to rub masking tape against the surface. **Far right.** Paint pulls away where rubber cement had been applied.

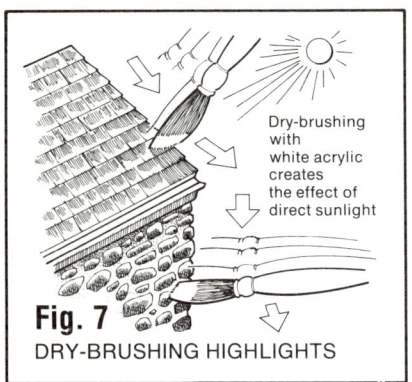

Fig. 7 DRY-BRUSHING HIGHLIGHTS

Fig. 8. Right. To make bases for buildings Malcolm first builds up with Styrofoam, then cements on surgical gauze, using white glue. **Far right.** He finishes the base with plaster, working in steps, small retaining walls, and other details.

ter and paint it over the brick surface, making sure to work it into the recessed mortar lines. Almost immediately, before the paint has a chance to dry, I wipe the brick surface lightly, leaving the recessed mortar lines filled with white. Because the Polly-S tends to dry quickly, I work only a small area at a time. I let the building dry for at least another hour before going on with construction.

WEATHERING METHODS

For much of my weathering I like to use pastel chalks, as shown in fig. 5. First I rub the sticks against sandpaper or a file to grind off a little dust onto a piece of paper. Next I brush the dust on the building with a soft brush. Earth tones such as Umber and Sienna — both the raw and burnt flavors — are good for representing grit and dirt.

I streak on gray dust to simulate rain stains, adding a little black here and there to vary the color. Once I'm satisfied with the look, I seal the dust to the building by spraying the surface lightly with Testor's Dullcote.

For that windblown dusty effect, I like to dump dry, real dirt over the sides of a building and blow off the excess. A light tan seems to work best for this effect. Dullcote also works fine for sealing dirt.

Next comes detail weathering. For rust stains around downspouts or pipe junctions I use thinned Floquil Rust. Thinned black is good for soot around smokestacks. I have a file of color slides showing weathering effects, and running through these helps me visualize the effects I want. Looking at the real world doesn't hurt either. Sometimes it's good to take a walk or a ride and just practice the art of seeing. Carry a camera and you can make a lasting record of your impressions.

Turning to the area of special effects, the old rubber cement trick, shown in fig. 6, is a good one for getting that peeled-paint look. First you texture the surface, then paint it a flat gray or tan and let it dry. Dab on patches of rubber cement. After the cement is dry, spray-paint the building whatever color you choose and let the paint cure for about an hour. Pick off the rubber cement with masking tape and — Ta-Da! — you have splotches of peeled paint with those ragged edges associated with the real thing.

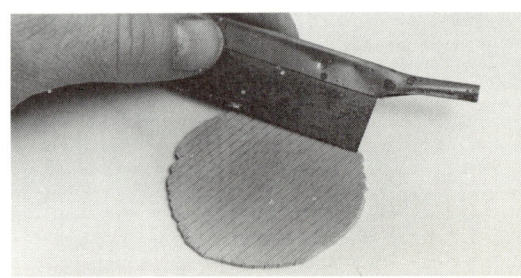

Fig. 9. Left. This backwoods water tank began with an AHM kit. Malcolm topped the brick base with a stripwood deck. **Above.** The new tank is a 2"-diameter mailing tube wrapped with Campbell's corrugated metal secured by contact cement. **Below.** Malcolm used a razor-saw blade to work some extra texture into the scribed tank top. **Right.** The spout and other kit parts complete the job.

Fig. 10. Left. Malcolm's friend, Craig Kosinski, kitbashed O'Burn's Mill. **Above.** He started out the project with a Tyco freighthouse kit. He sawed off the one-story portion, turned it 90 degrees, gave it a flat roof, and put the assembly atop a stone foundation. The stairs and railings are from the Tyco railroad hotel used for the Prairie Fire Inn.

FINISHING TOUCHES

Because our models are viewed under diffuse and relatively dim artificial light, we need to help them along if they are to look as if they are being struck by sunlight. I used the drybrushing technique illustrated in fig. 7. After dipping just the tip of a stiff-bristled artist's brush in white acrylic, I pull it through a paper towel to remove almost all of the paint, then stroke lightly on those parts I want to highlight. It's important not to overdo it. Just a little white along the edges of protruding bricks and cornices will add relief to the structure and help pop out the detail.

After the structure is painted and weathered, I add the windows. I like to use clear sheet acrylic for glass, sanding it lightly on both sides with fine sandpaper. This gives the glass a fogged look I like. Sometimes I add shades cut from colored construction paper and glued to the back of the windows.

Posters are a nice finishing touch and can be put about anywhere you'd like a dash of color. Some of the posters should be weathered and worn. You can paste newer posters over the old, being sure to let some of the old show.

Once you've finished construction of a building you're ready to place it on the layout. I like to build up plaster bases for my structures, as shown in fig. 8. In fact, the plaster finish coats on these bases are about the only plaster you'll find on the San Juan Central.

SOME SPECIAL STRUCTURES

Let's take a closer look at some of the structures on the SJC. Figure 9 shows the water tower next to the Montrose turntable. The brick base is from a Tyco kit, but for an entirely different look I replaced the Tyco tank with a scratch-built one. My tank is really just a mailing tube wrapped with Campbell's corrugated roofing material.

The O'Burn Lumber Co., shown in fig. 10, is the work of my friend, Craig Kosinski. He did an ol' switch-a-roo with the walls from the Tyco freight station kit to come up with this one-of-a-kind woodworking mill.

Trucks bound for O'Burn's get there via the old right-of-way and an old wooden-truss deck bridge left over from the 2-foot-gauge railroad that once ran through these parts. I made the bridge by flipping over a Campbell through-truss and cementing on wood strips to make a deck. See fig. 11.

The wildest town on the SJC is Tincup, a bawdy frontier town built on booze, broads, gold, silver, and old mine tailings — a Butch Cassidy sort of town. It *has* to be filled with outlaws. Most of Tincup shows up in figs. 3 and 12. I had a lot of fun putting this one together. The Tincup depot is another Kosinski kitbash, and it just reeks with Old West gingerbread and nostalgia! Shortening the long freight section from a Rico station converted it into a smaller structure that better fit the area.

Fig. 11. Above. The road bridge near O'Burn's Mill is an old railroad bridge left over from the days when a 2-foot-gauge railroad served the area. Malcolm cut into the Styrofoam scenery with a kitchen knife to work in the road. **Right.** Wooden railings and lots of detail complete the scene.

I built the Kalmbach Bull Shippers cattle pens from scratch, but Campbell's cattle pen kit would fit with a little rearranging. The cattle are by Dyna-Models — they even make a Texas Longhorn steer!

I built the railroad hotel from castings John Olson gave me awhile back. A structure that would probably work even better because of its split-level design is the Perkins Produce kit by Durango Press.

Across the tracks from the hotel is a structure no little rough-neckin' town should be without, the jail. Ours is a scratchbuilt effort by David Akin. Dave carved the walls in linoleum and made an RTV (room-temperature-vulcanizing) rubber mold so he could cast them in plaster.

On the backside of Tincup you'll find the McClanahan Mining Co. It's just a straightforward Campbell ore bin, but it did give me a chance to make some rusted and beat-up roofing by dipping pieces of Campbell's corrugated metal in the acid Radio Shack sells for etching circuit boards.

CROSSING THE CHASMS

Model railroaders have always liked their bridges, and I think I may like them even more than most. Certainly they add a lot of drama to a layout. The San Juan Central has plenty of bridges, and a good variety of them too. Fortunately, most of them are simpler to build than they look. In Chapter 7 we'll look at how to build them, including the rickety wood trestle over the Rio Grande River shown on the opposite page. ◊

Fig. 12. Tincup station is a shortened kit. The tender-on-stilts water tower is a simple kitbash that would make a good project for many model railroads.

Bridges for the San Juan Central

SAN JUAN CENTRAL 7

A variety of spans adds spice to our colorful Colorado railroad

BRIDGES — they bring so much excitement to both real and model railroading. When I decided to model the rugged and romantic Colorado mountain country on the HOn3 San Juan Central I knew it would mean building lots of bridges, and that was just fine with me. Far from being a modeling problem, every opportunity for a bridge is an opportunity for dramatic scenes and photos, especially when we can model deep canyons that allow us to get down low and look up at the bridges and the trains crossing them.

It's hard to say what makes bridges so fascinating. Maybe it's the thrill of leaving the ground behind and almost flying. Maybe it's the extra little element of danger that always comes with crossing a bridge. Whatever it is, it's something people have always responded to.

For economy's sake a real railroad would probably settle on as few standard bridge designs as possible, but then real railroads aren't much interested in creating exciting photo possibilities just to please railfans. On the San Juan Central I wanted as much variety as I could get. I wanted bridges that were dramatic yet didn't overpower everything else. As with all other elements on the SJC, I wanted the bridges to contribute to the scene, not overpower it. Achieving good results without too much effort was also important — the goal was to build an entire model railroad that smacked of Colorado narrow gauge, not create superdetailed, contest-quality individual models.

TWO LITTLE, ONE BIG, AND A STONE ARCH

Little bridges are important too, and I needed several of them where Placer Creek cut through Montrose Yard. See figs. 1 and 2. Just about any railroad could use some little fellows like these, and they're great to warm up on before moving on to something bigger.

Figure 3 shows a much more ambitious effort, the long bridge where the main line crosses above itself at Montrose. A steel through-truss seemed just right for this location. The bridge is big enough to be imposing and complicated enough to be interesting, yet it doesn't overpower the buildings and the rest of the scene.

Fig. 1. Above. To build this simple bridge across Placer Creek, Malcolm first cemented a piece of cardstock under the track. Then he added a 12″ x 12″ wooden beam on each side. **Right.** He ballasted the deck and added simple railings. Painting them white added a bright touch to Montrose Yard.

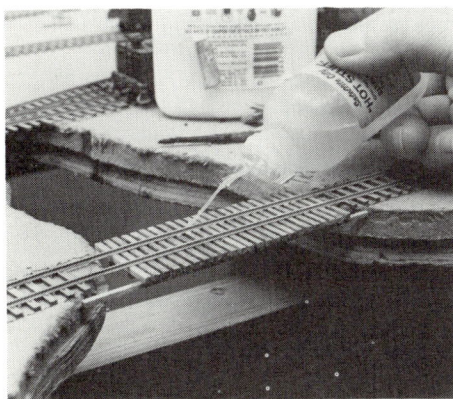 

Fig. 2. Above. To make the larger bridge spanning Placer Creek, Malcolm first removed the plastic ties under the rails. He replaced them with longer and more closely spaced wooden ties. **Right.** The wooden A frames with wire truss rods add a lot of character to make this an eyecatching little model.

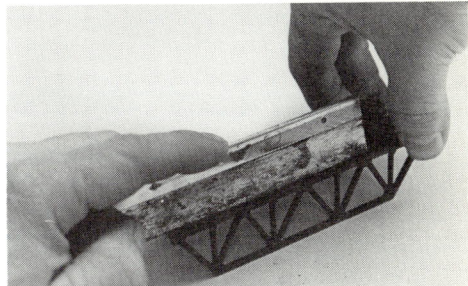
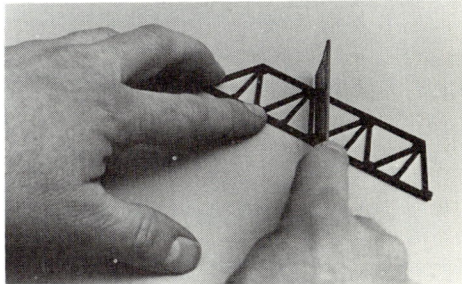
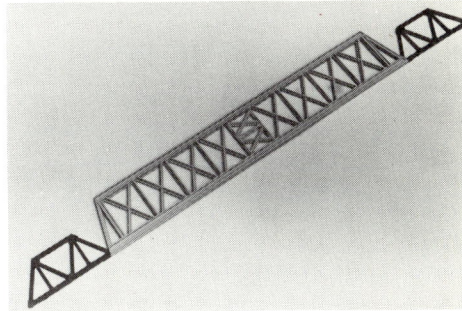

Fig. 3. Top. Malcolm made the long through-girder bridge at Montrose from a Heljan no. 1763 bridge kit and an Atlas no. 83 Warren truss. **Second down.** He cut the sides off the Atlas bridge with a razor saw. **Third down.** Each Atlas bridge side was cut up to yield two small approach bridge sides. **Fourth down.** Malcolm epoxied the short approach bridges to the ends of the Heljan bridge sides. **Above.** He made the deck from sheet styrene and glued on ties made from .040″ x .080″ styrene strip, spacing them about ¼″ apart. **Left.** Ooops. The trestle bent to support the near approach bridge would have fallen directly on the lower track. Malcolm found a neat solution; he moved both approach bridges to the far end.

 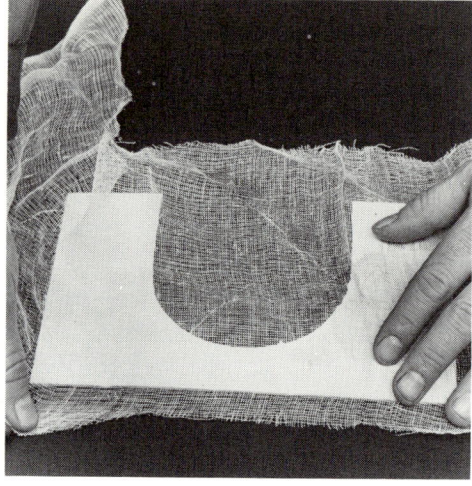 

Fig. 4. Above. The first step in making the stone arch bridge was cutting the sides from heavy cardboard. The coffee can made a convenient pattern. **Above center.** Malcolm glued on surgical gauze to give the plaster something to grip. **Above right.** He glued and stapled the bridge sides to the subroadbed.

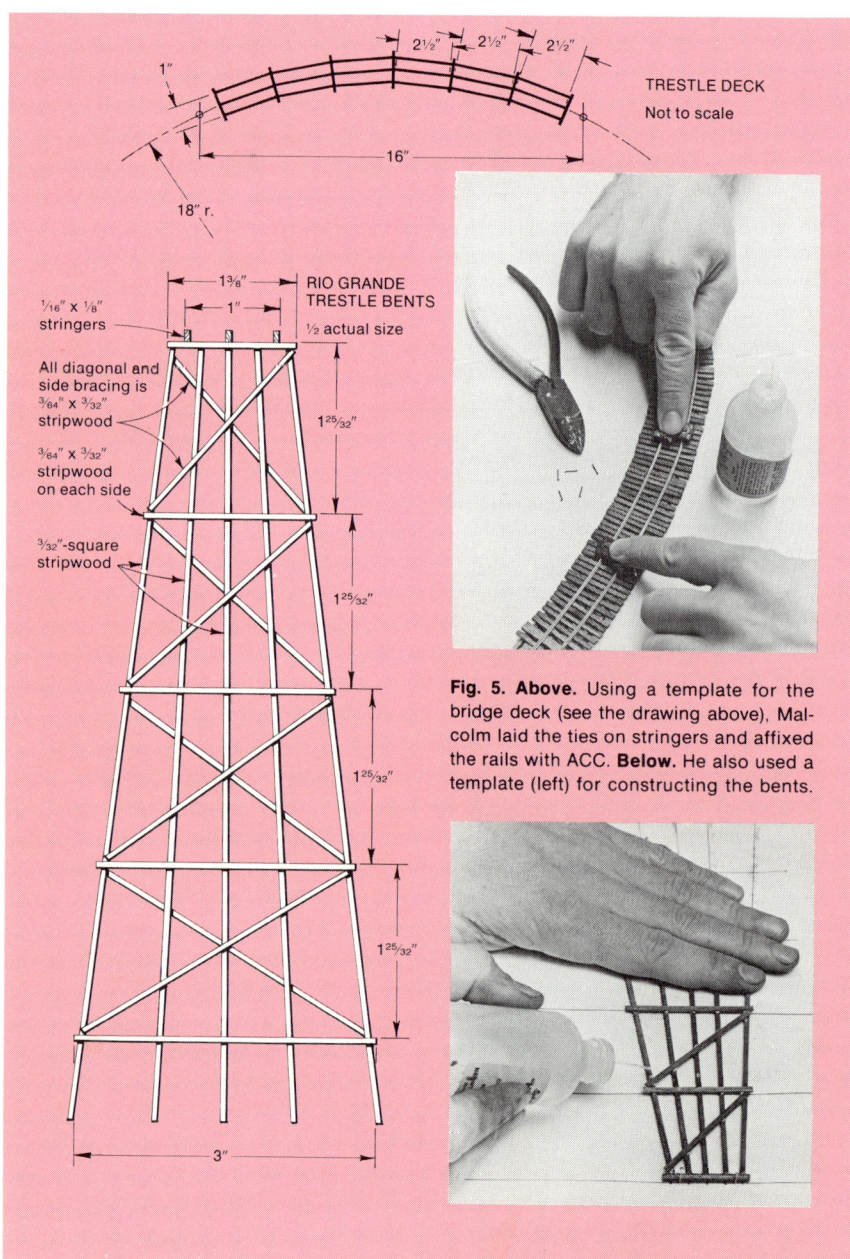

Fig. 5. Above. Using a template for the bridge deck (see the drawing above), Malcolm laid the ties on stringers and affixed the rails with ACC. **Below.** He also used a template (left) for constructing the bents.

Fig. 6 Above. Having built the bents at the workbench, Malcolm then plugged them into the Styrofoam base.

Follow the photos if you feel your version of the SJC needs a bridge like mine — it goes together fast and is fun to construct. If another type of bridge better suits your taste, go with that. Alternatives could be a wooden trestle or a series of Campbell's wooden through-trusses. Don't be afraid to make a mistake — I did. You've heard of those "best laid plans of mice and men." Well, as you can see from the photos, I had to change my bridge before I could install it, otherwise I'd have had a pier right in the middle of the railroad track!

I have a real passion for stone arch bridges — especially after seeing photos of those magnificent soaring structures that the late John Allen built on his

 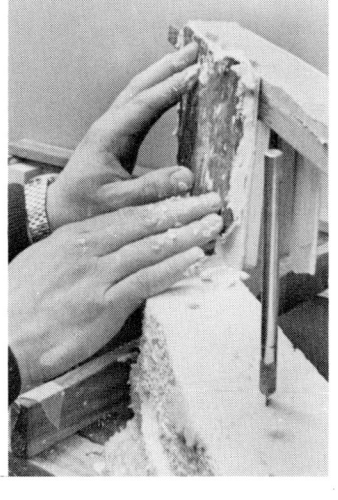  

Above. Next came the strip of cardboard which formed the inside of the arch.
Above right. Malcolm cast the bridge with one of his retaining wall molds.

Above. Once the plaster set, but before it could harden, Malcolm trimmed out the opening. **Above right.** A final detail was carving in the arch stones.

Above. With all bents in position and cemented to the deck over Rio Grande Canyon, Malcolm added the horizontal bracing that ties the bents together.

Above. The finished trestle defined the shape of the front of the Rio Grande section, and the rest of the scenery in this area derived naturally from it.

Gorre & Daphetid. The arch bridge on the SJC was simple to build using the techniques shown in fig. 4. It was just a matter of putting up a plaster rock wall and knocking a proper hole in it. Incidentally, this was one of those very few instances where I used plaster on the layout. Probably you could make the bridge with foam, using the foam rock casting techniques I discussed in Chapter 5.

THE RIO GRANDE TRESTLE

I wanted the long, curved timber trestle on the Rio Grande section to be tall and spindly. The color photo at the beginning of this chapter gives you a good, closeup look at it. Among model railroaders bridges like this must be the all-time favorite. It's great armchair adventure to imagine yourself seated in an old-time coach and looking way down into a canyon as you swing into space on a swaying, creaking trestle.

A trestle like this may look as if it would be very time-consuming and difficult to build, but really it isn't. Making major assemblies at the workbench, as shown in fig. 5, makes the work easier, and I was able to build the trestle in only a couple of evenings. Prestaining all the wood saves time and makes for a neater job. If you try to stain after finishing the job, you'll run across glue spots that won't take the stain. It also helps to mass-produce and stockpile the various lengths of timbers you'll be using before starting assembly.

To make a trestle like mine the first thing you'll need is a template for laying out the deck. You can draw such a template directly on a piece of Homasote, using the dimensions included in fig. 5.

Using ordinary straight pins, pin the three stringers to the Homasote. Locate the outside stringers so they fall closely under the two rails. You guys who used to build model airplanes will realize it's a good idea to put waxed paper over your template so you don't glue your bridge deck to it. Glue the ties to the stringers, spacing them closer than for normal track. Let the assembly dry thoroughly before proceeding.

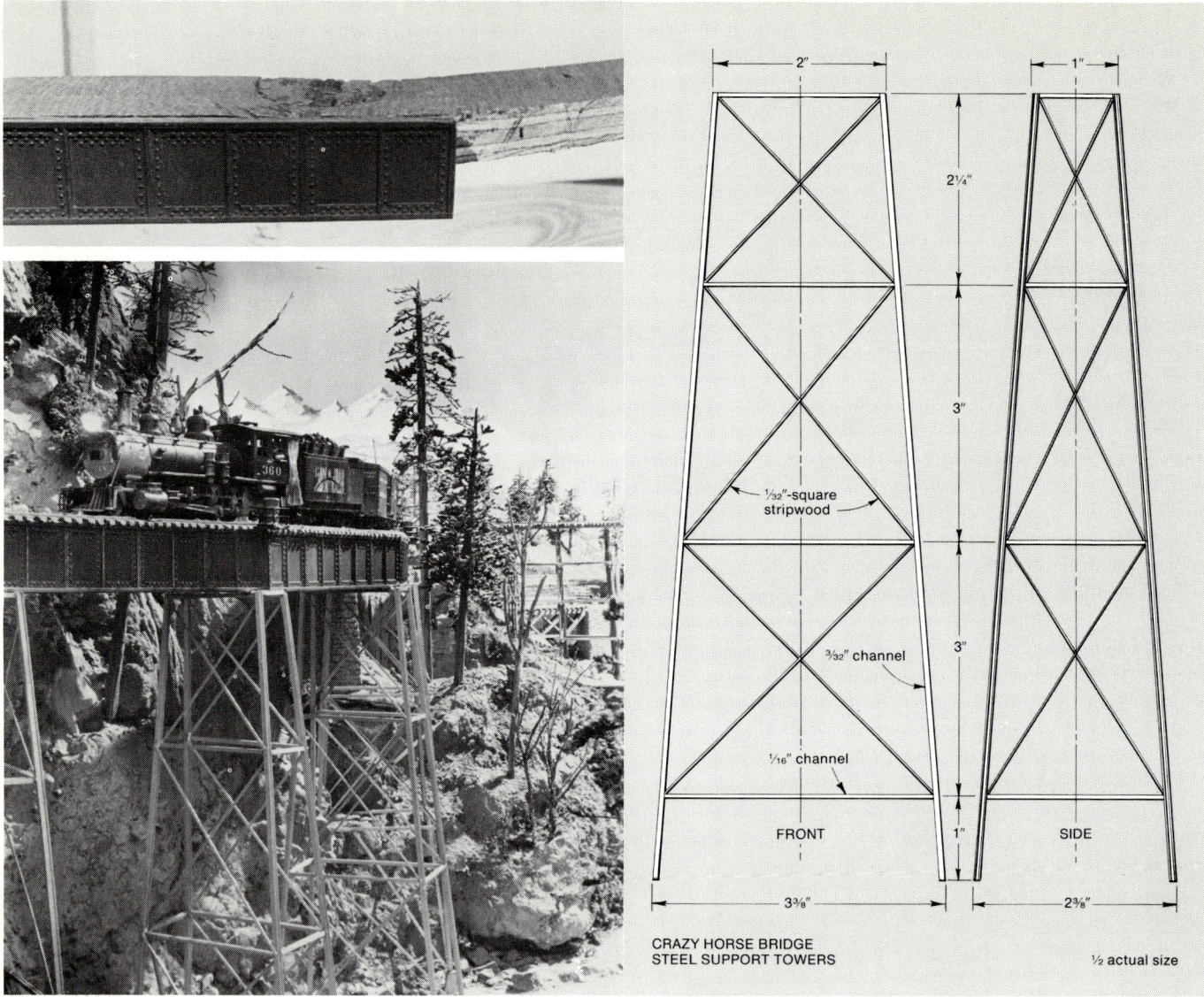

Fig. 7. Top. Malcolm made the deck for Crazy Horse Bridge by cementing segments of Atlas plastic girders to the plywood subroadbed. Atlas sells these to be used as flatcar loads. **Above.** The bents were made from Northeastern wood Ts and channels. Plastruct shapes could also be used.

Next position a piece of flexible track with its middle on the deck and carefully bend it to shape. Remove the plastic ties from the portion that falls on the bridge, but leave them on at each end. Extending the track beyond the ends of the bridge will give you smoother transitions when you install the deck later. The end of a bridge is no place to have rail joints if you can possibly avoid them.

I had no problem securing the rails to the deck. First I put white glue all along the underside of both rails. I positioned the track on the deck, established a smooth curve on the outside rail, and set this rail with ACC. Then, starting at one end and using a pair of gauges, I worked the inside rail into position, fixed it in place with ACC, and spiked it. Next I installed the deck on the layout. See fig. 6.

As the photos show, my Rio Grande Canyon didn't exist at this point. Remember, *you* know where you're going — I didn't have that luxury. Using the sheet foam techniques I described in Chapter 5, I soon had a valley to cross.

Instead of building the trestle bents first and then creating the scenery to fit them, I thought it would be more practical (and more realistic) to establish the geology first, then create the trestle as an engineering solution. This is the way it always happened on the prototype — they never went out of their way to build a trestle just because it was pretty to look at!

Building the bents moved swiftly and easily. Once again I used a template. You can use your hand as a gluing clamp or you can put in extra effort and build a jig. Since there are relatively few bents on this trestle, I forewent the jig.

CRAZY HORSE BRIDGE

Figure 7 shows how I built Crazy Horse bridge. Incidentally, at one point a large rock formation almost overhangs this bridge. That rock is my tribute to Mother Grundy, a famous formation on the Denver, South Park & Pacific. The original got its name because its shape reminded train riders of a woman's profile.

Crazy Horse is a spindly steel trestle engineered out of plywood, Atlas plastic girder flatcar loads, and bents made from wood shapes. I purposely made the bents flimsy to give the bridge that "hope the train makes it over" look. No great mathematical formulas were used here — I improvised out of the desire to create a dramatic scene. What really counts is the vertical distances involved, the mountain rearing up on one side and the canyon dropping away on the other. Again, I wanted the scenery to overpower the structure. Judge for yourself from the color picture on the opposite page whether it worked (the fog effect, by the way, was done for the photo with dry ice).

That's it for actually building the railroad. I've given you the basics, and I'm sure you can decipher a lot of the details by looking at the photographs. Next we'll take a look at completing the illusion with appropriate rolling stock. The emphasis will be on weathering and modeling the signs of hard use. ✥

San Juan Central 8

Locomotives and cars for the San Juan Central

Fig. 1. Left and above. Malcolm built both SJC steamers from Model Die Casting kits. He weathered them with colored chalk powder applied with a soft brush.

With weathering techniques for building a roster with character

IT'S HIGH TIME we assembled and detailed some locomotives and cars for the HOn3 San Juan Central we've been building. Compared to the HO standard gauge equipment most of us are familiar with, this 3-foot-gauge rolling stock is really tiny, and that big difference in size is an important part of why I like narrow gauge so much. You can get a lot of railroading into a small space, and it's a brand of railroading loaded with enough character and charm to make up for the smaller size of the equipment!

The cars and engines of Colorado's narrow gauge railroads may have been small, but they proved to be durable indeed, in some cases even lasting to the present. Nor was luxury unknown to those who rode the little trains in the Rockies. Some narrow gauge passenger equipment was as opulent as anything you might have found on the mighty New York Central, "out East."

LOCOMOTIVES

You have to have some engines if you want to pull some trains, so let's look at the SJC's roster. A lot of HOn3 motive power is available, mostly in relatively costly brass models imported from Japan and Korea, and eventually you may want to add one or two of these to your stable. However, Model Die Casting has come to the rescue of those wanting to get started in narrow gauge on a relatively small budget. That company offers two very fine HOn3 steam locomotive kits featuring styrene body parts on a metal chassis.

Both MDC engines are 2-8-0 Consolidations, but one has an outside frame and the other an inside frame. Given their relatively low price, under $50, I decided to purchase one of each for the SJC. Both are shown in fig. 1. These engines are based on general 3-foot practice rather than following specific prototypes, although the outside-frame engine closely resembles the Crystal River C-25, and the inside-frame engine looks a lot like a Denver & Rio Grande Western C-21 class locomotive.

You can assemble the MDC locomotives as per the instructions and they'll run just fine. You can also make one or two modifications to alter their appearance and improve the running qualities. I used Patco's kit for lowering the boilers to give that low-slung look usually associated with narrow gauge steamers. Jim Eakin explained how to perform this same modification in the October 1979 issue of MODEL RAILROADER magazine.

Patco also offers a regearing kit to slow down the locomotives, but I chose a remotoring-and-gears set from NorthWest Short Line. I like to use can motors to power my engines, and Sagami makes a really good one. That's what's included in the NWSL kit.

WEATHERING

Now that we have our coal-burners nearly fired up, let's make them look like they've slogged up a few hills and conquered a few miles of slim gauge railroad — I'm talking weathering.

First, I like to spray a little Floquil Grimy Black over an engine to effect a smidge of weathering and at the same time tone down that glowing styrene sheen. The Grimy Black gives me a flatter surface with some tooth to it, and I next reach into the chalkbox and start adding some powdered colors that will add character to the SJC mudhens. A little gray here, some rust there, and a final dry-brush session with white can really help pop out the detail and character of a locomotive.

A bit of extra detailing can help too. Add some piping, change an air pump, and so on if you desire. Prototype photos are a great source of ideas here. Cab curtains like those shown in fig. 2 can give a custom look. These curtains helped

Fig. 2. Malcolm attached tissue cab curtains with white glue and painted them with thinned black.

Fig. 3. Malcolm made his narrow gauge Gorre & Daphetid combine, left, by sawing strips from the ends. He continued these cuts through the bottom of the car, then cemented it back together. The roof was narrowed by sawing off the outside edges. Tissue paper represents tarpaper roofing.

keep the crew warm while they worked through the cold mountain winters. To represent them fold some tissue accordian-style and weather it a bit with Grimy Black and Dio-Sol. Punch or tear a few holes in the curtains and they'll look as if they've been burned or torn by rough use.

To add a touch of color I paint the smokebox with Floquil's Old Silver and weather it with some black chalk dust applied with a brush. To represent calcium deposits on the dome, I first wet it with water then brush on some streaks of white chalk dust. For dry-brushing on highlights I use Floquil's Polly-S White.

ROLLING STOCK

With the engines ready to haul, let's consider our consist. Cars used by Western narrow gauge roads were mostly constructed out of wood with metal hardware. Most tank cars used metal for the tank itself, although sometimes the tank rode on a wooden flatcar. Flatcars were most often wooden, although the closing years of the narrow gauge era saw the 6000-series standard gauge metal flats used on the D&RGW.

Years of rugged service took their toll, and by the 1930s the rolling stock began

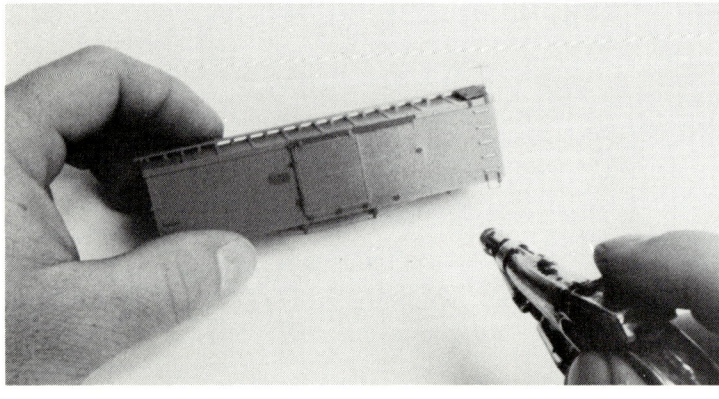

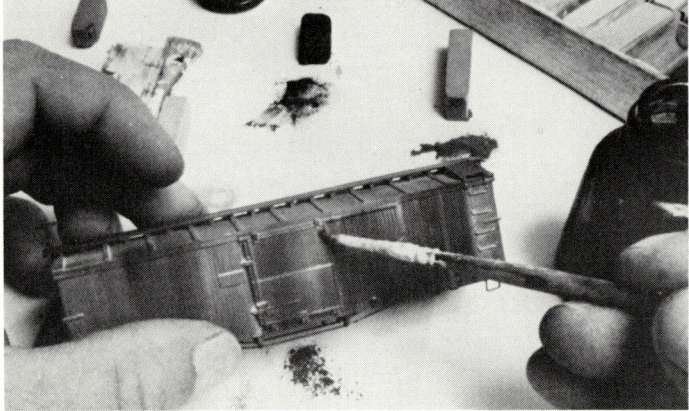
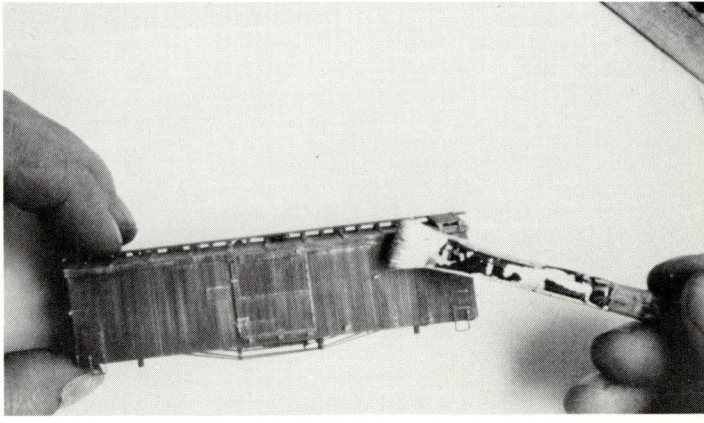

Fig. 4. Above left. First step in finishing a car is applying a color base coat, using an airbrush. **Above middle.** Careful work with an X-acto knife creates some battered boards. **Above right.** Powdered chalk is brushed onto the car and fixed with a clear spray. **Below left.** A touch of thinned Grimy Black to hardware helps bring out its detail. **Below middle.** Malcolm dry-brushes everything, including the trucks and couplers, with white. **Below right.** For the ultimate in a used look, the author goes to his dirt-dipping technique, scrabbling the car in a box of dirt and fixing the results with a clear spray.

to show its age with broken boards, humped or swayed spines (depending on the tightness of the truss rods), and flaking paint and faded lettering. Such cars offer interesting modeling subjects far removed from the fast-paced diesel age we live in now.

A wealth of narrow gauge cars are available in kit form for slim-gaugers working in HOn3, so sample a few and see where your preferences lie.

My Gorre & Daphetid combination baggage and passenger car, shown in fig. 3, turned out to be an interesting kitbash, starting with a Model Die Casting standard gauge car. I just narrowed the car, slipped on a pair of Pacific Fast Mail passenger trucks, and watched her roll, a neat model for about 10 bucks. Your kitbashed combine should be together in about two evenings of work.

The Rio Grande had 3000-series boxcars strung out all over the mountains of Colorado, and I've used the wooden kits from Alamosa Car Shops for several of these. They feature a built-up body to which detail parts are attached. You can assemble a couple of kits in an evening. I also like the Rail Line plastic kit, which takes a bit longer to construct, but which results in a very precise miniature of the real thing.

I like to use Kadee's no. 714 HO couplers, although some narrow gaugers prefer N scale couplers. Grandt Line trucks offer great detail and they roll well under your SJC freight cars.

Fig. 5. This trio of equipment ranges from a freshly shopped car to one that's been on its last leg so long no one can remember when it wasn't. Malcolm built the swayback car by distorting the plastic parts in a 200-degree oven before assembling them. Battered edges on a wood hopper can be carved in with a knife. A hot soldering iron is good for working dents and battered edges into plastic cars.

WEATHERING FREIGHT CARS

After you've assembled a few cars for the SJC, you'll want to study photos of prototype narrow gauge rolling stock for weathering ideas.

Figure 4 shows some of my techniques for finishing a car. I particularly like the effects I get by applying chalk dust to the car sides and roof with a soft-bristle brush. Airbrushing on weathering effects is also an excellent method, but chalks are just as subtle, are easier to apply, and are more forgiving of error. If you don't like what you see, blow it off and start over. Once you've achieved the look you're after, make it permanent by spraying the car with Testor's Dull Cote. Dry-brushing with Polly-S White helps pop out the detail.

Those stockcars need a little hay on the decks, and you can use macrame fibers to simulate this. Also add some white lime deposits to represent traces of the disinfectant used to wash out the cars. Why not put a few sheep or cattle in the cars for detail? I used the stockcar kit from E&B Valley for the SJC and populated the interior with Campbell cattle.

The sway-backed gondola shown in fig. 5 is a good example of the peeled-paint look you can get using rubber cement. First I gave the car a base coat of Floquil's Driftwood Gray. When the base coat was dry, I dabbed on patches of rubber cement and sprayed the car Grimy Black. Once this coat had dried I used masking tape to pull off the paint over the rubber cement and let that gray weathered wood show through.

By now you probably have the hang of it and are developing some weathering techniques of your own. There's no patented technique for this part of the hobby, and I certainly don't do every car the same way. The important things are to experiment and to use whatever techniques work well for you.

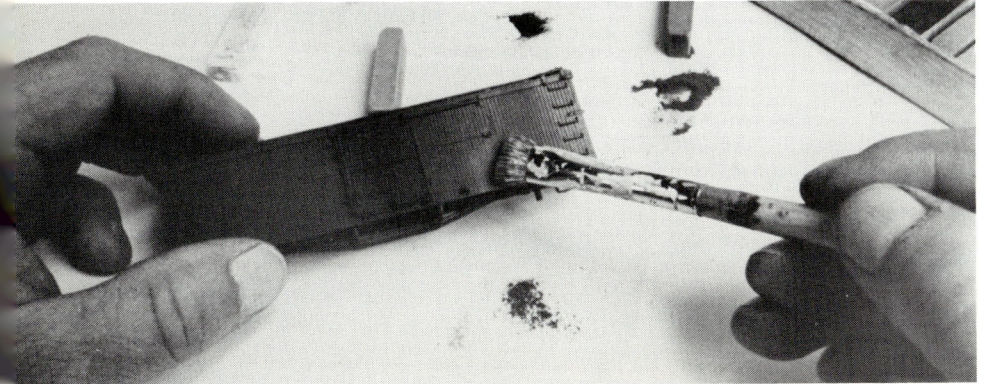

READY TO ROLL

Let's see, we've got the track in and working, the wiring's complete, the scenery is looking pretty good, and the structures and detailing are coming together. Why don't we take a few of the cars we've been assembling and make up a train? Better yet, let's scratch our heads and come up with an operating scheme for some real fun on the San Juan Central. That'll be the subject of our final chapter.

Operation offers an opportunity for friends to get together. It's nice if the layout is finished, but not essential. Steele Craver, left, runs a train while author looks on. Right is John Romberger.

SAN JUAN CENTRAL 9

Operation on the San Juan Central

This Card Pocket System could be tailored to just about any model railroad

BUILDING a model railroad is always great fun, and completing the San Juan Central was a real accomplishment for me, but what happens after all the mountains, track, rivers, and roads have found their place? Well, as that old model railroad saying goes, a layout is never actually finished. You can always add detail, add or subtract track, revise the scenery, or build craftsman-type kits to replace quickly constructed, less-detailed plastic items.

As your skills improve you'll want to go back and perform surgery on areas needing your new talents. I know my home layout, the Denver & Rio Chama Western, manages to undergo a change or two now and then — kind of like keeping the "groove" as the rock musicians say.

But there's another "groove" to this hobby of model railroading — operation! No, I don't mean firing up the transformer and blasting over the main line, but actually putting our trains to work and running a model railroad like the real thing. Sure, we have to make certain concessions because we are dealing with illusion to a large degree, but operation sure can enhance the overall enjoyment of the hobby.

CONNECTIONS TO THE WORLD

If we exercise the imagination a bit, we can break the bounds of our train room or basement. We can imagine that our HOn3 San Juan Central is really a north-south bridge route with connections to the world, rather than a loop of track on an 8 x 10-foot layout. See fig. 1. (To make our "prototype" map work we pretend Tincup isn't there the first time we go through it.)

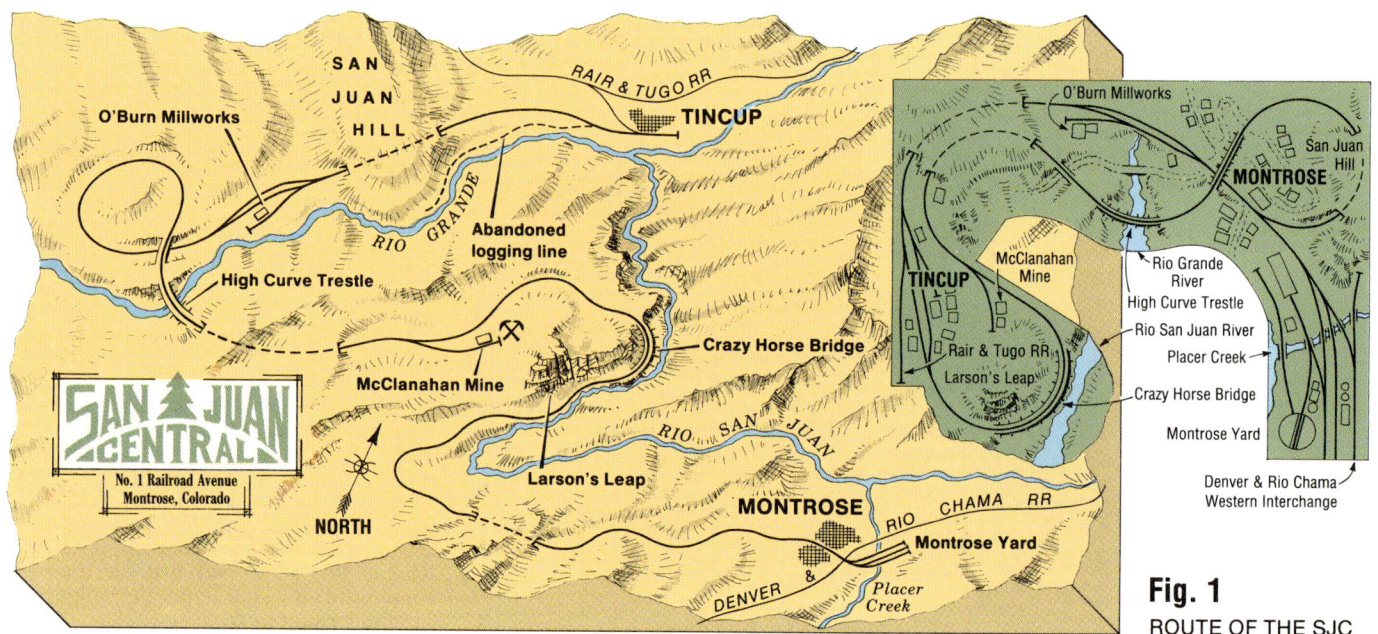

Fig. 1
ROUTE OF THE SJC

54

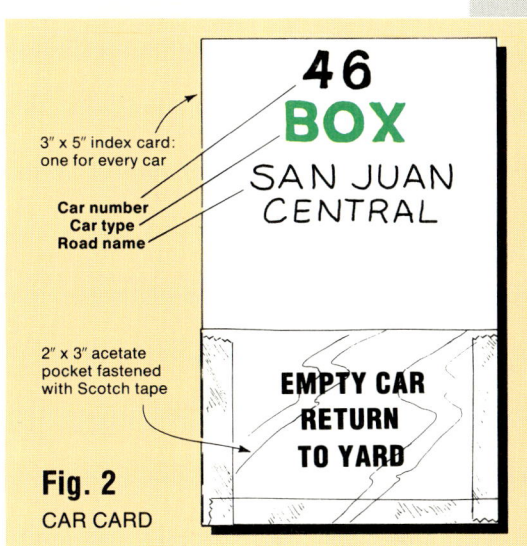

Fig. 2 CAR CARD

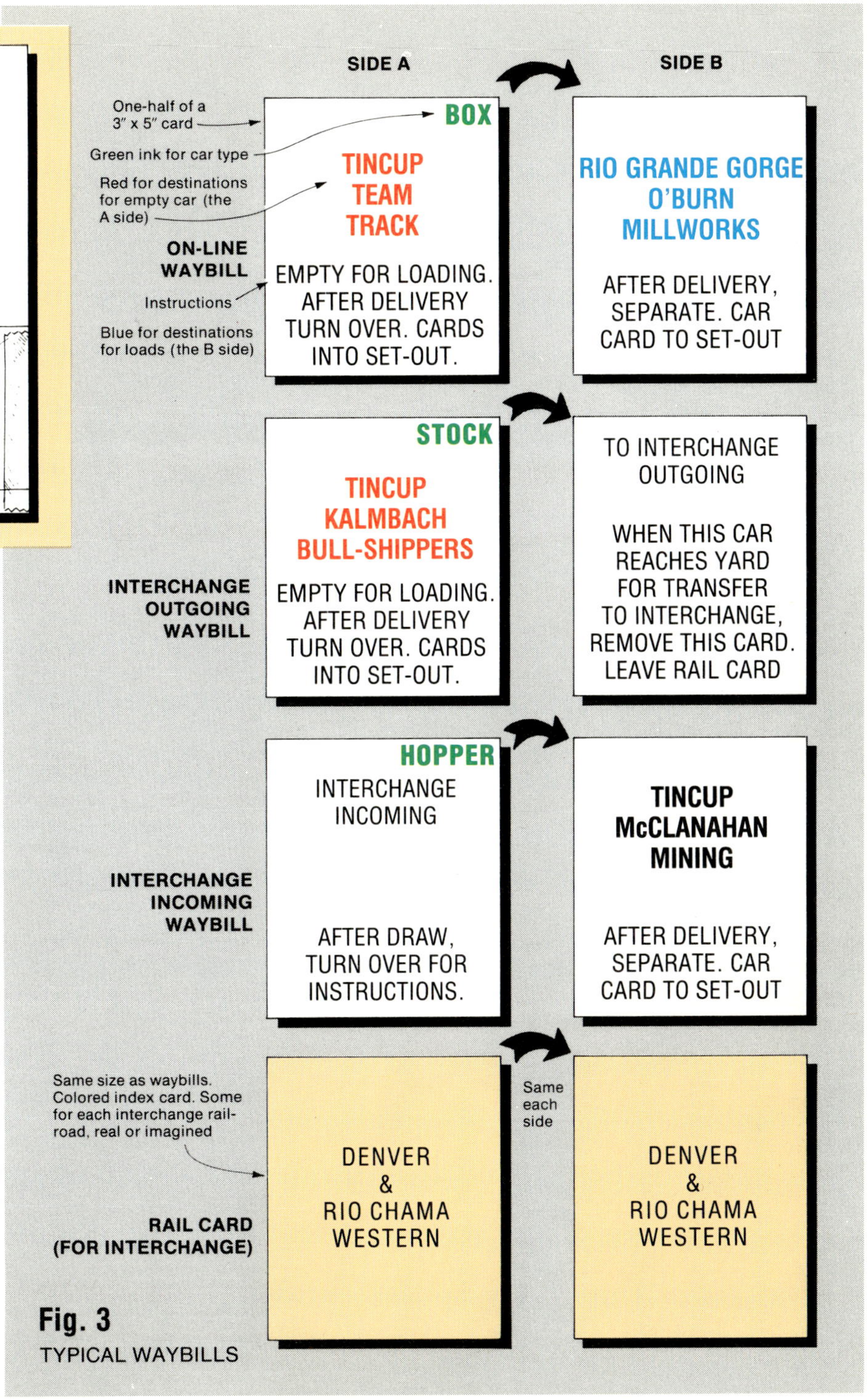

Fig. 3 TYPICAL WAYBILLS

Interchanges are vital to achieving this "beyond the layout" feel, and they are especially important for a layout as small as the SJC. I have two interchanges, one at Montrose and one at Tincup. Interchanges let us take cars on and off the railroad and provide justification for different road names appearing on the pike. Also, they can be used for car storage, sort of like an auxiliary yard.

The interchange concept was shown to me by Wally Kosinski, who uses it on his Sleepy Valley Lines. There's always a different way to do something, and I've tailored his interchange system to fit the needs of the San Juan Central.

A CARD POCKET SYSTEM

Operation can be simple, or complicated, depending on how you like it. Some famous pikes are operated using a fast-time clock to make train movements more interesting (and sometimes more hectic!). But I like a system that's a bit relaxed, kind of like the old narrow gauge lines themselves. The method I use on the San Juan Central I refer to as the Card Pocket System.

This Card Pocket System is based on operating systems developed over the years by many authors that have contributed to MODEL RAILROADER. As the ball's been bounced back and forth, different ideas have modified the system so that it's become more-or-less generic.

HOW THE SYSTEM WORKS

I'll start out by explaining how the system works in general, then I'll get into the specifics. For each car in the train there's a car card that the engineer carries along with him. On each card is a clear plastic pocket. A smaller card placed in that pocket tells the operator what to do.

Once the operator completes the prescribed move he leaves the card in a set-out box mounted on the layout's edge. The next operator to come along will look at the card and move the car where it goes next.

Now let's take a more detailed look at the system, starting with the cards.

• **Car Cards.** Every car you want included in working trains must have a car card that goes everywhere with it. I make my car cards from 3" x 5" index cards, as shown in fig. 2. On the lower half I print the instruction, "Empty car, return to yard." For this and much of the rest of my card lettering I use a rubber stamp with changeable type. These are available at rubber stamp stores; you can locate one in larger towns by looking in the Yellow Pages under Rubber Stamps.

Each card has a clear plastic pocket held on with Scotch tape. These pockets hold the waybills, which we'll get to in a minute. Obviously, when the waybills are removed we'll see the "return to yard" instruction.

On the top half of each car card I print the car's road name, number, and type (box, tank, flat, etc).

• **On-line waybills.** These cards, illustrated in fig. 3, go in the plastic pockets on the car cards and tell the operator where to take the car. You can think of them as representing orders from shippers wanting to do business. My waybills measure 2½" x 3"; I make them by cutting 3" x 5" cards in two.

The cards are lettered on both sides. Side A represents a call from a particu-

lar industry for an empty car. Side B tells where the car is to go after it has been loaded.

There's a lot of duplication on these cards, so besides doing a neat job, the rubber stamp can also save time. You can use colored inks as an aid. I use green for car types, red for destinations for empties (the A side), and blue for destinations for loads (the B side).

Figure 4 shows how an on-line waybill works. Take a minute to look it over. It's really very simple — each operator just follows the instruction on the card and is concerned with only one move.

• **Interchange waybills.** To spice up the action and make it more realistic I have also incorporated two kinds of interchange waybills: incoming and outgoing. These are also shown in fig. 3.

Side A of an outgoing interchange waybill is just like side A of an on-line waybill. Side B, though, says "To interchange, outgoing." When you get this instruction you don't go directly to an interchange, but instead go back to the yard where the dispatcher (that's usually you again) processes the car's paperwork, an operation that consists simply of removing the waybill and replacing it with a rail card.

• **Rail Cards** represent interchanges. The SJC has two, one with my Denver & Rio Chama and the other with Craig Kosinski's Rair & Tugo.

My rail cards are the same size as waybills, 2½" x 3", but I made them from colored cardstock to contrast with the white stock used for the waybills. All they have written on them is the interchange's name. I have five cards for each interchange.

To route an outgoing interchange car, just draw a rail card at random and insert it in the car card's pocket. The car is then put on the next train and delivered to the interchange spur.

In real life the neighboring railroad would then switch the car into a train and take it out into the world. In the case of a model railroad, we haul the car away with the old 0-5-0 (pick it up with our hand) and put it on a storage shelf.

• **Incoming interchange waybills.** To bring a car onto the layout we draw an interchange incoming card and match it with a car on our storage shelf. Side A of an incoming interchange card is illustrated in fig. 3. The B side is the same as the B side for a regular waybill.

To determine which interchange we'll come in on, we draw from our rail cards again. We set the car on the interchange spur and place the waybill in the transparent pocket. The next train along will take the car to the yard. Once there we'll turn over the waybill to reveal the car's destination, and it will be switched out on the next train.

ESTABLISHING THE TRAFFIC

The traffic patterns on your railroad will depend on how many and what kinds of cards you make. If, for example, you make three times as many waybills for one industry as you do another, that industry will, over the long run, get three times as much traffic. Once you've had a few operating sessions you can readjust the system's flow by adding or removing waybills.

You can also establish and adjust the traffic between industries. I did it by setting up a grid on an awfully large sheet of paper with the names of each industry and interchange along each axis. My original is long lost, but an experimental version to help get you started is shown in fig. 5. You'll soon find yourself making changes in it.

To determine my traffic patterns I compared the industries to each other, and with a twisted sense of logic, determined what car types the industries would order and where they would send them once they were loaded. I had fun with this by making hypothetical explanations of what might be in the cars. O'Burn's Millworks, for example, might periodically ship a load of new chairs to Hayden's Hideaway to replace those broken in brawls. These cars would be set out on the team track in Tincup.

THE SYSTEM IN ACTION

Now that we've made our cards, let's make some money for the SJC:

• Empty cars are in the yard and our little teakettles are excited about being put into revenue service. The trainmaster, that's you, has all his paperwork in order. An operator shuffles the deck of waybills and draws off eight cards to use in making up his three-car train. (Three-car trains are standard on the SJC because of the steep grades and short passing sidings.)

He looks at the waybills and sees which moves are feasible or preferred. One card, for example, might call for a tank car, but there's none in the yard. The card goes back in the deck. The only flatcar might be buried deep in a holding track. Better move on to the next card, as digging out the flat would hold up the other operators. Maybe a car is already spotted at the industry calling for one, so there'd be no place to spot the empty.

• The engineer throttles his engine around the yard, making up the train. He finds the car cards that correspond to the cars he's picked up and places the waybills in the plastic pockets.

• To give the sensation of travel, the engineer builds up some mileage by looping around the circuit before going to work.

• Once the initial loop is completed, the engineer looks at his orders and drops off cars and cards at the appropriate industries along the line. If there are any cars to be picked up at the interchanges, he fetches those and brings them and their cards back to the yard for in-processing.

• If two or more are operating, the second train can begin assembly as soon as the first train has left the yard.

The action can get mighty interesting when two or more operators are running at the same time. On such a small layout they're bound to get in each other's way — negotiation and cooperation become a must. The PSI command control system makes for even more fun. The trains operate completely independent of one another with no track power block assignments to worry about. You could even have some cornfield meets!

END OF THE RUN

I said before that there's an old model railroad saying about layouts never being finished. However, books about them must be, and we've come to the end of the San Juan Central story. I hope you've enjoyed it. It's been fun, but best of all, the fun doesn't have to end here. After all, fun is just another name for operation.

Fig. 5 EXPERIMENTAL TRAFFIC FLOW CHART
*Incoming Interchange — Interchange used is determined by random draw of rail card

FROM (A side of waybills) / TO (B side of waybills)

CAR CODE
B = Box
T = Tank
H = Hopper
G = Gondola
F = Flatcar
S = Stockcar

FROM \ TO	INTERCHANGE	MONTROSE YARD	Montrose Freighthouse	Montrose Findley Fuel	Montrose Team track	McClanahan Mine	O'Burn Millworks	Tincup Station	Tincup Team track	Tincup Kalmbach Bull-shippers
INTERCHANGE	■	All interchange cars	3B	2T	2B 1F	3H	2B 1F 1T	3B 1F	3B 1F	3S
MONTROSE YARD	All interchange cars	■	7B	4T	5B 1F	5H	1B 1F 1G	4B 1G	4B 1F	4S
Montrose Freighthouse	2B	All empties	■	X	X	1B	1B	1B	1B	1B
Montrose Findley Fuel	2T		X	■	X	1T	1T	X	X	X
Montrose Team track	2B 1F		X	X	■	1B	1B	1B	1B	1B
McClanahan Mine	3H		X	X	X	■	1H	X	1H	X
O'Burn Millworks	2B 1F		1B	X	1B	1B	■	X	1B	X
Tincup Station	1B		1G	X	X	1B	1B	■	1B	X
Tincup Team track	1B		1B	X	1B	X	1B	X	■	X
Tincup Kalmbach Bull-shippers	3S		X	X	X	X	X	X	X	■

ACKNOWLEDGMENTS

The 12 months or so that it took to build the San Juan Central were exciting, and finishing the railroad was truly an exciting experience. Then seeing the final product of all that model railroading fun culminate into a magazine series and now a book has added a special reward to a special project.

Along with all of the fun (and, at times, hard work) that I had designing and building this narrow gauge pike, others had a lot of fun working on the railroad, too. Friends both here in Texas and in other parts of the country lent their expertise, both physical and mental, helping me solve the problems inherent in building what amounts to a medium-sized home layout in only one year. I want to thank everyone who helped, even though there isn't room to mention all of them by name.

Craig Kosinski pulled me through when I was sure that I had bitten off more than I could chew. Craig is an excellent modeler, typist, confidant, and kitbasher extraordinare. His magic with structures is evident in the depot at Tincup and O'Burn's Millworks. Craig also lent a hand in formulating the finished look that the San Juan Central displays — just count the pine trees!

Dave Akin — the "Sn3 kid" of Dallas — helped me install the Dynatrol receivers in the SJC locomotives, and more than once counseled me on my photographic efforts. Dave had a lot to do with producing the "fog shots" at Crazy Horse Bridge.

Steele Craver, who's literally a walking museum of narrow gauge information, helped me in areas of slim gauge manners (or should I call it decorum?). "This will work," "that won't work," and "they always did this," were among Steele's famous San Juan Central quotes.

John Romberger, not me, actually built the little gold-belted steamer (No. 361) for the San Juan Central's motive power roster. When on "business" trips to Dallas, John would always stop by to contribute both constructive criticism and a helping hand. With luck, his boss won't ever read this page!

Jim Findley's late-night tales of John Allen and his Gorre & Daphetid railroad fired my imagination and inspired a magic mainline that led straight to my heart.

John Olson made an important indirect contribution to the SJC — it was one of John's magazine articles that got me into model railroading. I blame all of this on him.

Ol' Johnny "O" once said that "hobby shops are the lifeblood of model railroading," and I heartily agree. Special thanks go out to the M. A. L. Hobby Shop in Irving, Texas, and to Loryn Abrams at Hall's Hobby House in Dallas. Further from home, Fred Hill of The Original Whistle Stop in Pasadena, California, contributed some of his undying spirit for our hobby, and all the folks at William K. Walthers Inc. in Milwaukee, Wisconsin, and at Lambert Associates in San Leandro, California, helped find kits, parts, and materials for the SJC.

I can't believe that Sharon Furlow, my wife and friend for 20 years, let me start the construction of the SJC in my own son Shawn's bedroom (after I had moved Shawn to another part of the house — how about the breakfast room!). Sharon displayed extraordinary restraint in not throwing me and the layout out of the house in the dead of winter! She even made contributions throughout the project with constructive criticism like "What's that supposed to be?" and "When will it be finished?" (You see folks, I already have one other layout.) Sharon also helped with photography and scenery, served as a third and fourth hand, and sometimes even catered the affair. Sharon — can I move back in now? It's almost winter again!

Billy Michael Haynes is my cousin, and a great photographer. He helped with some of the photos, including the front cover of this book. Bill (he's too old for me to call him Billy) is an artist with the camera.

And thanks go, too, to Bill Haynes Jr. (my grandfather), John A. Haynes (Uncle John), and Uncle Bill Haynes Sr. All worked for the old Texas & Pacific, and through them I received my rich railroad heritage and my love for the romance of America's steam era.

My son Shawn never knew what hit him when I moved into his room — lock, stock, and barrel — to construct the SJC. Through it all, he never complained, and usually greeted me and my work on the layout with "Hey man — lookin' good!" Eventually the railroad moved out, and I've since built an upstairs studio where the SJC was finished. Shawn, you can have your room back, and thanks.

Wally Kosinski, Craig Kosinski's dad, helped me put together the operating scheme for the San Juan Central. Thanks for a great job.

My late father, Malcolm Furlow Sr., and my mother never discouraged me from being a dreamer, because without dreams our realities sometimes suffer. They bought me my first train — an American Flyer.

DEDICATION

The story of the San Juan Central is dedicated to the late Bill McClanahan. Along with John Allen, Linn Westcott, and others, Bill pushed the hobby to an art form. Bill forever inspired the hearts of model railroaders with his work, his humor, and his guidance, and his work continues to inspire me.

SUPPLIER ADDRESSES

When you're building a model railroad, even a modest one like the San Juan Central, finding the specific products you need is a big part of the project. Here are the addresses for the manufacturers of the hobby products used on the San Juan Central.

Be sure to check with your local hobby shops before writing to the supplier. William K. Walthers, Inc., also listed below, issues a large HO catalog each year and conducts a mail-order business. Walthers is perhaps your best bet for locating hard-to-find products.

AHM structures
Regal Way
451 East Tioga Street
Philadelphia, PA 19134

Alamosa Car Shops
12157 Valliant Drive
San Antonio, TX 78216

Anderson turnout links
Earl Eschleman
53 Maytown Avenue
Elizabethtown, PA 17022

Atlas Tool Co., Inc.
378 Florence Avenue
Hillside, NJ 07205

A-West
P. O. Box 1144
Woodstock, GA 30188

Caboose Industries
1861 North Ridge Drive
Freeport, IL 61032

Campbell Scale Models
P. O. Box 121
Tustin, CA 92680

Chooch Enterprises, Inc.
P. O. Box 217
Redmond, WA 98052

Durango Press
P. O. Box 1836
Lynnwood, WA 98036

Dyna-Model Products Co.
RFD Box 624
Sangerville, ME 04479

E & B Valley cars
Eastern Car Works, Inc.
P. O. Box 804
Richboro, PA 18954

Floquil-Polly S Color Corp.
Route 30 North
Amsterdam, NY 12010

Grandt Line Products
1040B Shary Court
Concord, CA 94518

Heljan structures
imported by JMC
1025 Industrial Drive
Bensenville, IL 60106-1297

Kadee Quality Products Co.
720 South Grape
Medford, OR 97501

Kalmbach Video
1027 North Seventh Street
Milwaukee, WI 53233

Magnuson Models Inc.
Div. Wm. K. Walthers, Inc.
5601 West Florist Avenue
Milwaukee, WI 53218

Mann-Made Products
P. O. Box 27009
Cincinnati, OH 45227

Model Die Casting Inc.
3811-15 West Rosecrans Avenue
P. O. Box 926
Hawthorne, CA 90250

Model Power
180 Smith Street
Farmingdale, Long Island, NY 11735

Modeltronics
21751 Santa Bella Place
Cupertino, CA 95014

Mountains in Minutes
6008 Alexa Lane
Sylvania, OH 43560

N. J. International, Inc.
77 West Nicholai Street
Hicksville, NY 11801

NMRA
(National Model Railroad Association)
4121 Cromwell Road
Chattanooga, TN 37421

Northeastern Scale Models Inc.
P. O. Box 727
Methuen, MA 01844

NorthWest Short Line
Box 423
Seattle, WA 98111

Pactra Industries
420 South 11th Street
Upland, CA 91786

Patco
5711 Florin-Perkins Road
Sacramento, CA 95828

Power Systems Inc.
56 Bellis Circle
Cambridge, MA 02140

Rail Line
3600 Pittman Road
Independence, MO 64052

The Rock Quarry
P. O. Box 26372
Dallas, TX 75226

Sculptamold
American Art Clay Company
4717 West 16th Street
Indianapolis, IN 46222

Sequoia Scale Models
1760 Monrovia, A-15
Costa Mesa, CA 92627

Shinohara track
imported by Lambert Associates
5 Town & Country Village, No. 782
San Jose, CA 95128

Terminal Hobby Shop
5619 West Florist Avenue
Milwaukee, WI 53218

Tyco Industries
6000 Midlantic Drive
Mt. Laurel, NJ 08054

Wm. K. Walthers, Inc.
5601 West Florist Avenue
Milwaukee, WI 53218

Woodland Scenics
P. O. Box 98
Linn Creek, MO 65052

Thomas A. Yorke Enterprises
P. O. Box 1330
Fontana, CA 92335

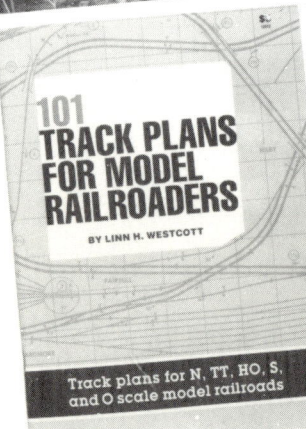